GETTING AND SPENDING:
The Consumer's Dilemma

GETTING AND SPENDING:
The Consumer's Dilemma

Advisory Editor
Leon Stein

The Public Accepts

STORIES BEHIND FAMOUS TRADE-MARKS
NAMES AND SLOGANS

I[saac] E. Lambert

ARNO PRESS
A New York Times Company
1976

Editorial Supervision: EVE NELSON

———◆———

Reprint Edition 1976 by Arno Press Inc.

Reprinted from a copy in
  The Newark Public Library

GETTING AND SPENDING: The Consumer's Dilemma
ISBN for complete set: 0-405-08005-0
See last pages of this volume for titles.

Manufactured in the United States of America

———◆———

Library of Congress Cataloging in Publication Data

Lambert, Isaac E   1890-
    The public accepts.

    (Getting and spending)
    Reprint of the ed. published by University of
New Mexico Press, Albuquerque.
    1. Trade-marks--United States. 2. Slogans.
3. Business names--United States. I. Title.
II. Series.
[T223.V2L3 1976]   658.8'27   75-39256
ISBN 0-405-08029-8

The Public Accepts

The Public Accepts

STORIES BEHIND FAMOUS TRADE-MARKS
NAMES AND SLOGANS

By
I. E. LAMBERT

Introduction by
WILLIAM ALLEN WHITE

PUBLISHED BY
THE UNIVERSITY OF NEW MEXICO PRESS
ALBUQUERQUE, N. M.

*This book is dedicated to the
American advertiser who has
faith in his product and pride
in his name*

PREFACE

THE AUTHOR has selected for his collection of stories famous American trade-marks, names, and slogans, which he believes have received public acceptance. These stories reflect an important part of the business development of this country. The origin of many date back to the Gay Nineties and other expansion eras when America was making industrial history. There are many other well-known trade-marks, names, and slogans, but space does not permit the inclusion of all.

A trade-mark is a symbol, word, or mark used by one who manufactures or sells goods, to distinguish them from similar goods made or sold by another. It has reference to the things sold, and it is usually applied to products sent into the market.

A trade name is a name which is used in trade to designate the business or goods of a particular trader. Generally a trade-mark is applicable to a vendible commodity, and a trade name to business and goodwill. The names, however, are frequently confused, but the same fundamental principles are applicable to both, and the terms are sometimes treated by courts as substantially synonymous.[1]

A phrase may be associated by usage with a business or goods. Such a phrase is commonly referred to

[1] American Steel Foundries v. Robertson, 269 U. S. 372, 46 S. Ct. 160, 70 L. Ed. 317.

as a slogan. America always has been phrase-minded, and the public responds to pungent expressions, e. g.:

"It's wise to be thrifty"—*Benjamin Franklin*
"Give me liberty or give me death"—*Patrick Henry*
"A house divided against itself cannot stand"—
Abraham Lincoln
"Go west, young man, go west"—*Horace Greeley*

As public opinion has been sold by famous sayings of this character, so has the purchasing public been sold by certain well-known trade slogans.

ACKNOWLEDGMENT

THE AUTHOR wishes to express his appreciation to the executives of the various companies owning trademarks, names, and slogans who have coöperated in furnishing data which have made this book possible.

CONTENTS

Page

Introduction by William Allen White 17

Trade-mark No. 1 19

His Master's Voice 23
(Radio Corporation of America)

Ask the Man Who Owns One 27
(Packard Motor Car Company)

Uneeda Biscuit 29
(National Biscuit Company)

All the News That's Fit to Print 31
(*The New York Times*)

Kodak 33
(Eastman Kodak Company)

Good to the Last Drop 35
(General Foods Corporation)

Flying Red Horse 37
(Socony-Vacuum Oil Company, Inc.)

Eventually, Why Not Now? 39
(The General Mills, Inc.)

La Belle Chocolatiere 41
(General Foods Corporation)

Coca-Cola 43
(The Coca-Cola Company)

Leo, the Lion 45
(Metro-Goldwyn-Mayer)

Ivory Soap 49
(Proctor and Gamble Company)

Mr. Peanut 51
(Planters Nut and Chocolate Company)

Monk's Foot 53
(American Felt Company)

John B. Stetson 55
(John B. Stetson Company)

Aunt Jemima 57
(The Quaker Oats Company)

Waterman's 59
(L. E. Waterman Company)

CONTENTS (Continued)

Page

The Beer That Made Milwaukee Famous 61₄
(Jos. Schlitz Brewing Company)

Benjamin Franklin Head 63
(The Curtis Publishing Company)

Munsingwear 65
(Munsingwear, Inc.)

A & P 67
(The Great Atlantic and Pacific Tea Company)

Bicycle Playing Cards 69
(The United States Playing Card Company)

Gillette 71
(Gillette Safety Razor Company)

When It Rains It Pours 73
(Morton Salt Company)

Community Plate 75
(Oneida, Ltd.)

Keen Kutter 79
(Simmons Hardware Company)

Cover the Earth 81
(The Sherwin-Williams Co.)

Palm Beach 83
(Goodall Worsted Company)

Time to Re-tire "Get a Fisk" 85
(United States Rubber Company)

There's a Reason! 87
(General Foods Corporation)

Dutch Boy 89
(National Lead Company)

Louisville Slugger 91
(Hillerich and Bradsby Company)

The Shell 93
(Shell Oil Company)

Life Savers 95
(Life Savers Corporation)

Cellophane 97
(E. I. du Pont de Nemours & Company)

Cream of Wheat 99
(The Cream of Wheat Corporation)

Vaseline 101
(Chesebrough Manufacturing Company)

CONTENTS (Continued)

Page

Four Roses 103
(Frankfort Distilleries, Incorporated)

Arrow 105
(Cluett, Peabody & Company)

Colt 107
(Colt's Patent Fire Arms Manufacturing Company)

P. K. 109
(Wm. Wrigley Jr. Company)

Who's Your Tailor? 111
(Ed. V. Price & Co.)

Clicquot Eskimo 113
(Clicquot Club Company)

See America First 115
(Great Northern Railway Company)

The Bell Symbol 117
(American Telephone and Telegraph Company
and Associated Companies)

57 Varieties .... 119 +
(H. J. Heinz Company)

Walk-Over 121
(Geo. E. Keith Company)

1847 Rogers Bros. 123
(International Silver Company)

Mennen for Men .... 125 +
(The Mennen Company)

Carnation Milk "From Contented Cows" 127
(Carnation Company)

Sleep Like a Kitten 129
(Chesapeake and Ohio Lines)

Before You Invest—Investigate 131
(National Better Business Bureau, Inc.)

Hasn't Scratched Yet 133
(The Bon Ami Company)

Portland Cement 135

White Owl 137
(General Cigar Co., Inc.)

Tanglefoot 139
(The Tanglefoot Company)

Quaker Oats 141
(The Quaker Oats Company)

CONTENTS (Continued)

Page

Frigidaire 143
(General Motors Corporation)

Beautyrest 145
(Simmons Company)

Sunkist 147
(California Fruit Growers Exchange)

Going ! Going !! Gone !!! 149
(The Herpicide Co.)

Watch the Fords Go By 151
(Ford Motor Company)

White Rock 153
(White Rock Mineral Springs Company)

An Apple a Day 155

Body by Fisher 157
(General Motors Corporation)

Kotex
Kleenex 159
(International Cellucotton Products Co.)

Buster Brown 161
(Brown Shoe Company)

Ethyl Gasoline 163
(Ethyl Gasoline Corporation)

Old Dutch Cleanser 165
(The Cudahy Packing Company)

The Prudential Has the Strength of Gibraltar 167
(The Prudential Insurance Company of America)

Knox Gelatine 169
(Charles B. Knox Gelatine Co., Inc.)

Thomas A. Edison Signature 171
(Thomas A. Edison, Incorporated)

Listerine 173
(Lambert Pharmacal Company)

20 Mule Team 175
(Pacific Coast Borax Company)

Holeproof 177
(Holeproof Hosiery Co.)

Campbell Kids 179
(Campbell Soup Company)

The Watch That Made the Dollar Famous 181
(The Ingersoll-Waterbury Co.)

CONTENTS (Continued)

Page

606 183

Iron Fireman 185
(Iron Fireman Manufacturing Company)

The Ham What Am 187
(Armour and Company)

Rexall 189
(United Drug Company)

Log Cabin Syrup 191
(General Foods Corporation)

The Skin You Love to Touch 193
(Andrew Jergens Company)

Bakelite 195
(Bakelite Corporation)

Flit Soldier 197
(Stanco Inc.)

Bromo-Seltzer 199
(Emerson Drug Company)

Red Heart 201
(John Morrell & Co.)

Singer 203
(Singer Manufacturing Company)

The Greatest Name in Rubber
Wingfoot—The Goodyear Symbol 205
(The Goodyear Tire & Rubber Company, Inc.)

Truth in Advertising 209
(Advertising Federation of America)

Rock of Ages 211
(Rock of Ages Corporation)

Canada Dry 213
(Canada Dry Ginger Ale, Inc.)

Camel 215
(R. J. Reynolds Tobacco Company)

Don't Write—Telegraph 217
(Western Union Telegraph Company)

Piggly Wiggly 219
(Piggly Wiggly Corporation)

Paris
No Metal Can Touch You 221
(A. Stein & Company)

CONTENTS (Continued)

Page

The Red Cross Emblem 223
(Johnson & Johnson)

The GE Monogram 225
(General Electric Company)

Arm & Hammer 227
(Church & Dwight Co., Inc.)

Keep That Schoolgirl Complexion 229
(Colgate-Palmolive-Peet Company)

Bull Durham 231
(American Tobacco Company)

Toastmaster 235
(McGraw Electric Company)

Scripps-Howard Lighthouse 237
(Scripps-Howard Newspapers)

B. V. D. 239
(B. V. D. Corporation)

ASCAP 241
(American Society of Composers, Authors, and Publishers)

Give Whitman's Chocolates
It's the Thoughtful Thing to Do 243
(Stephen F. Whitman & Son, Inc.)

Greyhound 245
(The Greyhound Corporation)

The Watch of Railroad Accuracy 247
(Hamilton Watch Company)

Say It With Flowers 249

Smith Brothers 251
(Smith Brothers, Inc.)

INTRODUCTION

By WILLIAM ALLEN WHITE

THE PEOPLE of the United States being suggestible are easily hypnotized. A big noise, big type, high pretense, mob clamor moves a considerable part of the American people. It is the price democracy pays for literacy. The people of the United States believe what they hear, what they see, whatever is imposed upon them suddenly, persistently, or under the guise of authority. The spell is transitory. They wake up soon. But while they are waking from one spell, another is being woven about them. Fake advertising is always profitable in the short run and never in the long run. The words, "fire sale," or their equivalent, always lure Americans. But on the other hand, the hometown merchant, the regular advertiser, whose goods justify his advertising, has no trouble in finally outselling the "fire sale."

So advertising has become a thoroughly exact science. It has its quackeries, of course. But the man with a useful, necessary article, well-priced, well-serviced, and well-made, may depend upon scientific advertising as surely as he may depend upon rental values for his store when the site is chosen to fit his needs. Advertising pays. "The Public Accepts" the goods of the honest advertiser who has faith in his product and pride in his name.

Certain trade-marks, names, and slogans consistently used over a period of years have favorably impressed the American public. Their origins in many instances have been unique.

This book is a case record of good psychology. The man who studies this will know something about the American people. It is carefully edited, intelligently written. I commend it to those interested in advertising as a science and those psychologists who want to know how the wheels go round inside of the American mind. This book is worthy of any man's study who is wisely looking at the American scene.

TRADE-MARK NO. 1

No. 1
Reg. U. S. Pat. Off. October 25, 1870

As of January 1st, 1941, the records of the United States Patent Office disclose that 384,046 trade-marks have been registered. No. 1 trade-mark was registered by the Averill Chemical Paint Company, of New York City, a few months after the first Federal Trade-mark Law was passed in July, 1870.

The first law provided for the registration of trade-marks generally without regard to where they were used. The Act was held unconstitutional on the ground that Congress had no authority to regulate instruments of trade in intrastate commerce. In 1881, a new law was passed providing for the registration and protection of trade-marks used in interstate and foreign commerce. From time to time Congress has enacted various trade-mark laws. The two most important acts were passed in 1905 and 1920.

It is not necessary, however, to register a trade-mark in order to be entitled to protection. Registration simply constitutes prima facie evidence that the registrant is entitled to the mark. The purposes of trade-mark laws are to prevent confusion and to prohibit fraud and mistake. The right to a trade-mark exists at common law and has long been recognized and protected thereby. The origin of numerous trade-marks, names, and slogans set forth in this book antedate registration laws by many years.

STORIES BEHIND FAMOUS
TRADE-MARKS, NAMES, AND SLOGANS

HIS MASTER'S VOICE

Reg. U. S. Pat. Off.
Reproduced Courtesy of Radio Corporation of America

In 1924, newspapers all over the world published notices of the death of a man who, while not the world's most famous painter, can lay a strong claim to having painted perhaps the world's most famous picture. That is, if we may construe fame as meaning the picture that has been seen more often and is generally recognized by the greatest number of people.

Francis Barraud made no pretense at great eminence in the world of art. An Englishman, son and nephew of two well known British artists, his work —"His Master's Voice"—the little dog sitting before the horn of a talking machine, quizzically cocking a puzzled ear, is instantly identified in all corners of the world, in places where Michael Angelo and Da Vinci are strange names, and where even Coles Phillips and Maxfield Parrish are unknown.

"His Master's Voice" was not painted as a commission from any commercial organization. By the merest accident it became associated with large corporations. In the *Strand Magazine* of August, 1916, is told the story of "His Master's Voice":

Mr. Barraud, while in his London studio one day, noticed his little dog, Nipper, sitting in an attitude of puzzled interest in front of the horn of the talking machine in use at that time. Immediately the picture appealed to him as one which would strike a popular chord, and he painted it. Dissatisfied with the ugly black horn of the machine he had painted, Barraud, at the suggestion of a friend, asked the Gramophone Company, Ltd., to lend him a brass horn which would add color to his picture. The change was made, and company officials, realizing the value of such a picture to their business, bought the completed painting. The artist advised the Gramophone Company not to make it an obvious advertisement by putting their name across the background, but to leave it without any lettering and merely give it the title he had suggested, viz., "His Master's Voice," as the subject spoke for itself and required no explanation.

Long after the company had acquired the picture, the managing director instructed firemen, in case of a fire, to save first this original painting which hangs in the Board of Directors' room at the Gramophone Company's office in suburban London.

In the latter years of his life the artist was pensioned by the company which had purchased his painting.

An American organization, the Victor Talking Machine Company, early in its operations, secured the use of the picture and slogan, and later purchased controlling interest in the Gramophone Company. The growth of the Victor Company was phenomenal. "His Master's Voice" was prominently advertised with the famous name "Victrola" and Victor records.

Today the picture and slogan are owned by the Radio Corporation of America who thirteen years ago purchased the Victor Talking Machine Company. The officials of the Radio Corporation believed at that time, and still believe, "His Master's Voice" to be one of the Victor Company's most valuable assets. It is used extensively in the advertising of RCA products. Some midget radio sets are now called "Little Nippers," the name of the fox terrier portrayed in the picture.

ASK THE MAN WHO OWNS ONE

IN 1902, a young woman secretary held a letter before her employer and said: "This man asks for more information, for literature. He says he wants to know how he can be sure that the car we make is a good one." James Ward Packard stared out of the window a few moments, then swung around toward the waiting girl. "Tell him that we have no literature—we aren't that big yet. But if he wants to know how good an automobile the Packard is, tell him to ask the man who owns one." He then provided the prospect with the name of a Packard owner in his vicinity.

James Ward Packard little knew that this answer of his would become the slogan for one of America's best-known automobiles. He and his brother produced the first Packard car in a little electrical plant in Warren, Ohio, in November, 1899.

In the historical file of the Packard Motor Car Company there is a catalog dated 1903 which contains the first printed evidence of the slogan, "Ask the Man Who Owns One."

Many a manufacturer has a slogan for his product, but none is more consistently used than this one. For more than thirty-five years the Packard Motor Car Company has adhered to the unwritten rule that it should appear in every advertisement of a Packard car.

A simple, sincere answer became a famous slogan.

UNEEDA BISCUIT

Reg. U. S. Pat. Off.
Reproduced Courtesy of National Biscuit Company

THE NATIONAL Biscuit Company was organized in February, 1898. At that time crackers were sold in cracker barrels. As a rostrum for the village states-men the cracker barrel was not a bad idea, but it was a definite evil for the cracker industry. The shopping housewife, upon her return home, often opened her brown paper bag to find that she had purchased broken, stale, and dirty crackers.

Mr. Adolphus W. Green, chairman of the Board of the National Biscuit Company, conceived the idea of selling a fresh and clean soda cracker in a small, attractive package and giving the cracker a distinc-tive name as a remedy for the menace of the cracker barrel.

In August, 1898, a suggested list of possible names for the new product was submitted, such as "Hava Cracker," "Usa Cracker," "Taka Cracker," etc. The name "Uneeda" was also on this list, and finally, after some hesitation, it was adopted. The word "Uneeda" was probably the first coined combination of words which are so frequently used today for trade names.

In January, 1899, preparations were complete. One morning the people of Chicago and other Illinois cities woke to discover in the newspapers two mysterious words printed in bold type: "UNEEDA BISCUIT." This suggestive combination of letters aroused the curiosity of the purchasing public and the venture was a success almost overnight.

A few months later, Mr. Joseph J. Geisinger, seeking to illustrate the moisture-proof properties of the new package, dressed his young nephew, Gordon Stille, in boots, sou'wester, and slicker, put a package of "Uneeda Biscuit" under his arm, and took him to the photographer. When Mr. Green saw the result he was delighted. Thus the "Uneeda Boy" was added to the gallery of world famous trade-mark figures.

ALL THE NEWS THAT'S FIT TO PRINT

"SOUTH'S GREATEST Newspaper," "Strictly Independent," "Established in 1850," "Covers the Mississippi Valley"—compare these phrases which are so typical of the ones used by many newspapers in this country to the one used by THE NEW YORK TIMES, "All the News That's Fit to Print."

This phrase first appeared on the editorial page of THE NEW YORK TIMES October 25, 1896. The following February it was placed on the front page of the paper and has remained there ever since.

Probably no newspaper motto ever has aroused more discussion or more obstinate differences of opinion—a difference which was found in THE TIMES office as well as outside. The publisher, mindful of this controversy, offered a prize of $100 for any ten-word motto which seemed better to express the idea. Richard Watson Gilder, editor of the *Century,* was asked to act as judge in the contest which brought some 20,000 suggestions, of which 150 were thought good enough to publish. The prize was given to "All the World's News, but Not a School for Scandal"; but to the editors of THE TIMES this did not seem as satisfactory as their own motto, so, though the winner of the contest received his $100, "All the News That's Fit to Print" continued to be the motto of THE TIMES.

In its narrowest interpretation the phrase suggests

the offense often discussed under the title of "Suppression of News." No newspaper, however, prints all the news; for instance, the harrowing details of a sordid murder are often omitted, only the essential facts being published. The gruesome details can be left to the imagination.

"All the News That's Fit to Print" was a war cry, the slogan under which the reorganized TIMES fought for a footing in the nineties against the formidable competition of *The World, The Herald,* and *The Journal.*

Wide advertisement of its policy expressed in its motto contributed materially to the growth and standing of THE NEW YORK TIMES. This is an excellent example of the policy of an organization being incorporated in its slogan—"All the News That's Fit to Print."

KODAK

THE TRADE-MARK, "Kodak" was coined by Mr. George Eastman in 1888, at the time of his introduction of the No. 1 "Kodak." The origin of the word has run the gamut of human curiosity.

Mr. Eastman's own etymology of the word is contained in an interview:

"I devised the name myself. A trade-mark should be short, vigorous, incapable of being mispelled to an extent that will destroy its identity, and—in order to satisfy trade-mark laws—it must mean nothing. If the name has no dictionary definition, it must be associated only with your product and you will cease to be known as producing a 'kind' of anything.

"The letter 'K' had been a favorite with me—it seemed a strong, incisive sort of letter. Therefore, the word I wanted had to start with 'K.' Then it became a question of trying out a great number of combinations of letters that made words, starting and ending with 'K.' The word 'Kodak' is the result. Instead of merely making cameras and camera supplies, we make 'Kodaks' and 'Kodak' supplies. It became the distinctive word for our products."

Philologically, the word "Kodak" is as meaningless as a child's first "goo." Abrupt to the point of rudeness, bitten off by consonants at both ends, it snaps like a "Kodak" shutter.

The achievements of Mr. George Eastman and the

Eastman Kodak Company in research, manufacturing, and selling are well known to all. They have been the leaders of photography for more than fifty years.

The name "Kodak" is almost synonymous with camera, but the Eastman Kodak Company dispels the idea in the mind of the public that any camera is a "Kodak" by advertising "Only Eastman Makes the Kodak."

Mr. Eastman studied the dictionary in an endeavor to coin a word; now the dictionary contains the word he coined, "Kodak," with the following definition: "A trade-mark applied (originally) to a small hand camera. . . ."

GOOD TO THE LAST DROP!

"Good to the last drop"

Reg. U. S. Pat. Off.

Reproduced Courtesy of General Foods Corporation

JOEL CHEEK perfected the Maxwell House Coffee blend, and Theodore Roosevelt originated its famous slogan—"Good to the Last Drop!"

In 1907, when the President was visiting "The Hermitage," Andrew Jackson's old estate, he was invited to call upon Mr. Cheek at his home nearby. Naturally, Mr. Cheek served some of his coffee, of which he was very proud. After the President had finished drinking a cup of the coffee, the host asked his guest's opinion of the brew. "Good," cried President Roosevelt, with characteristic incisiveness, "good to the last drop!"

This slogan has been the cause of considerable correspondence from critical advertisement readers. Literally thousands of wags have written to the makers of Maxwell House Coffee wanting to know "what is the matter with the last drop?" Finally, the controversy was submitted to a well-known professor of English at Columbia University, who made a compilation of scores of quotations from the classics, proving that the use of "to" in this relation is inclusive and accepted good usage.

About sixty years ago in the Old South, Joel Creek was selling coffee over rough country roads on horseback. At the age of twenty-one he obtained a job as a salesman for a wholesale grocery house in Nashville, Tennessee. But his wares did not suit his own taste so he experimented with coffee blends. Having obtained a blend that satisfied him he quit his grocery job and joined partnership with J. W. Neal, and devoted his entire energy to the coffee business. He induced the management of the old Maxwell House in Nashville, which was famous throughout the South for the excellence of its cuisine, to try his coffee. As the weeks passed, the critical patrons of the old hostelry began to comment enthusiastically on the flavor of the new blend, and before long, the hotel decided they would serve no other. It was suggested that the coffee be called "Maxwell House," after the famous tavern, and the name was adopted.

Mr. Cheek and his partner, Mr. Neal, over the years that followed, built up a great enterprise, which joined the General Foods family in 1928.

FLYING RED HORSE

Reg. U. S. Pat. Off.
Reproduced Courtesy of Socony-Vacuum Oil Company, Inc.

THE "FLYING Red Horse," an adaptation of a trade-mark used for many years in foreign countries, has only comparatively recently made its appearance in the United States. It is associated with products of the Socony-Vacuum Oil Company, Inc., and its affiliates, and is today one of the most familiar trade-marks to the American motorist.

As far back as 1911, the "Flying Red Horse" was used abroad by the Standard Oil Company of New York and the Vacuum Oil Company affiliates. The Vacuum Oil Company of South Africa, Ltd., has used a flying horse as a trade-mark for nearly twenty-five years. It is a member of a rather large family of animal trade-marks used abroad—the cock in the Philippine Islands, the elephant in Indian and Egypt, the tiger in Japan, the stork in the Levant, and the monkey in India. In some lands, the trade-marks have religious significance. In others, the trade-marks were selected merely because they were distinctive and easily recognized and remembered by a trade to whom printed words meant little.

The "Flying Red Horse" is Pegasus of Greek mythology. There are various stories concerning him, and one of the best known states that when the Grecian hero, Perseus, cut off the Medusa's head the winged horse, Pegasus, sprang from the body, ascended into the abode of the gods, there to carry thunder and lightning for Zeus.

The "Flying Red Horse," signifying speed and power, which are the attributes of good gasoline, is a suitable emblem, and is among the most striking and artistic of present day trade-marks.

EVENTUALLY, WHY NOT NOW?

THE FIRST Washburn mill was built by Cadwallader C. Washburn, at St. Anthony Falls, Minneapolis, Minnesota, in 1866. Fourteen years later flour from Washburn mills was awarded the Gold Medal at the Millers' International Exhibition in Cincinnati, Ohio, thus marking the origin of "The Gold Medal" brand.

In 1907, Mr. Benjamin S. Bull—one of the earliest exponents of national advertising in American business—coined the well-known slogan, "Eventually, Why Not Now?" for Gold Medal Flour. In fact, the handwriting in which the slogan appears on the familiar Gold Medal Flour sack is his. There is a legendary story that Mr. Bull requested that certain members of his department submit catch phrases to be used for Gold Medal Flour. After many unworthy suggestions, Mr. Bull is supposed to have asked, "When are you going to give me a decent slogan?" His underlings stalled him off by saying, "Eventually," to which Mr. Bull thundered, "Eventually, why not now?"

The General Mills, Inc., the world's largest processor of wheat, is now the owner of the slogan, "Eventually, Why Not Now?" having acquired the slogan when it was organized in 1928 to take over the Washburn Crosby Company and several other milling companies.

LA BELLE CHOCOLATIERE

Reg. U. S. Pat. Off.
Reproduced Courtesy of General Foods Corporation

THE ORIGIN of one of the oldest and most famous trade-marks, "La Belle Chocolatiere," centers around a romance in the Austrian city of Vienna. Anna Baltauf, daughter of an impoverished knight, was a waitress in a chocolate cafe. She was slender and pretty. Into the cafe, one frosty afternoon in 1760, came Prince Ditrichstein, a gallant young Austrian nobleman, to sip a cup of the new beverage from the tropics—hot chocolate. The Prince was instantly attracted by the beautiful girl who waited on him. Day after day he returned for more chocolate and more glances at the charming waitress. The romance progressed and finally blossomed into marriage. As a bethrothal gift, the Prince engaged a talented Swiss artist, Jean Etienne Liotard, to paint his fiancee in the simple costume in which he first saw her. This portrait now hangs in the Dresden Museum—and its well known replica graces every can of Walter Baker's Breakfast Cocoa.

In 1780, Walter Baker & Company established the first chocolate mill in America at Dorchester, Massachusetts. This company is probably the oldest concern in the United States with a record of having made the same type of product continuously in the same location. Its chocolate products and Baker's Breakfast Cocoa are famous the world around.

The Baker Company and "La Belle Chocolatiere" joined General Foods in 1927.

COCA-COLA

"COCA-COLA" is one of the few trade-marks now in existence which have been recognized by the Supreme Court of the United States. In a decision in 1920 the Court said: "The name now characterizes a beverage to be had at almost any soda fountain."

In 1886, had one wandered into the kitchen of a certain old residence on Marietta Street, Atlanta, Georgia, one would have found at work there a man of mature years, an experimenter—Dr. J. S. Pemberton. He was not surrounded by the apparatus of a modern laboratory. His preparations were made in a kettle, measured with a ladle and stirred with a boat oar. He was not an expert, but a true experimenter, with faith in his idea of a perfect blend of flavors. Taste, not chemistry, was the test of the drink which he sought, and the human palate was his criterion. Every day, as he worked, he went to the corner drug store to try out his experiment. At the end of three years of labor, he had reached his goal, and his friend, Mr. F. M. Robinson, suggested that the drink be called "Coca-Cola."

The first year only twenty-five gallons were sold and $46 spent in advertising. Control of the drink passed from hand to hand. The founder died. The struggle attracted only slight local attention and "Coca-Cola" seemed destined to fade into oblivion. At this time, however, there stepped into the picture a man who was pleased with the taste and who had a vision of the future, Mr. Asa G. Candler, the owner of a small drug store on Peachtree Street, Atlanta. Mr. Candler first acquired a one-third interest in the business; then two-thirds; and finally, in 1891, he held the entire right to the formula, the trade-mark, the kettle, and the oar.

From 1892 to 1919, the story of "Coca-Cola" was the history of the business ingenuity of its owners— the Candler family. In 1919, however, the business was sold to The Coca-Cola Company, a Delaware corporation, and the stock was thrown open to public subscription.

When "Coca-Cola" appeared on the market there were only a few soda fountains in the United States which were open the year round. In some states there were none. Carbonated water was regarded by many as a medicine. "Coca-Cola" played a major role in making the soda fountain one of America's most distinguished institutions. It also contributed materially in developing the bottling industry.

It is doubtful if any trade-mark has been more widely advertised than "Coca-Cola." Various slogans have been used in connection with it from time to time; an outstanding one is the current phrase, "The Pause That Refreshes."

LEO, THE LION

Reg. U. S. Pat. Off.
Reproduced Courtesy of Metro-Goldwyn-Mayer

THE MOST famous trade-mark in the history of amusements is the Metro-Goldwyn-Mayer Lion, Leo. Known to millions, throughout the United States and Europe, it has a history and personality which extends from the days of the silent films to the present talkies and Technicolor.

The trade-mark was created by Howard Dietz, director of publicity and advertising for Metro-Goldwyn-Mayer, and one of the best-known publicists in the world.

In 1916, Dietz, then a student at Columbia University, left the classroom to join the Philip Goodman Advertising Agency. At that time, Goodman's clients included Samuel Goldwyn, who was chairman of the Board of Directors for Paramount Pictures, and who subsequently resigned his office to organize with Edgar Selwyn, Goldwyn Pictures, Inc.

Anxious to establish his new firm with the proper publicity, Goldwyn asked Goodman to prepare a suitable trade-mark; and Goodman, in turn, assigned the task to Dietz. The young man, still fresh from college and imbued with the ideals of his alma mater, chose Columbia University's Lion (symbol of courage) as a basis for his design. An artist named Morris Rosenbaum made the sketch and to this Dietz added the Latin inscription, "Ars Gratia Artis," which in practical translation means "Art for Art's Sake."

The resultant trade-mark was adopted with enthusiasm, and has long survived its original purpose. For when Goldwyn retired from the company to make way for the merger of Metropolitan with the interests of Louis B. Mayer, the Lion continued as a trade-mark.

With the advent of sound in the movies, Leo took on full leonine powers. He opened his mouth, blinked his eyes and emitted a growl. When someone would see a more imposing lion at the zoo, a new king of beasts would be photographed for a new title strip. Thus, the official Leos became so numerous that M-G-M finally decided to end the confusion with a story that the real Leo was to be taken back to Africa and released in the jungle. Intended as an humanitarian gesture, the yarn brought protests from animal lovers who declared that a lion reared in captivity would soon starve or be slain in the wilds. So Leo was supposed to be pensioned comfortably in a zoo for the rest of his days. Actually, however, nobody remembers which particular lion it was that posed for the current Metro trade-mark.

Few people attending a Columbia University football game and hearing the crowd sing "Roar, Lion, Roar," while the Columbia Lion prances about the field, realizes that this lion provided the inspiration for M-G-M's Leo, emblem of the world's greatest motion pictures.

IVORY SOAP

AT THE end of the seventies, Procter and Gamble were making soap in Cincinnati. The second generation of the firm was well in the saddle. At this time they were putting a new type of soap on the market— one that floated. A tradition is that the formula for this new product had been purchased from a young foreigner who had offered it to them as a means of producing a high grade of castile soap without using olive oil. Another account states that a workman, in a hurry to go to his lunch, had left his crutcher running, and upon his return he found that the soap had filled with air in tiny bubbles and that the bars made from this batch floated quite easily upon the surface of water. Still another story is that the floating character of the soap was not recognized until a dealer had ordered another case of "that soap that floats." Whatever the origin of the first batch, the result was that the makers recognized its interesting possibilities—and knew how to make it again.

The story of how the new soap came to be named is this: Harley T. Procter, a member of the firm, was seated one morning in a church when the following passage from the Psalms (45:8) caught his ear and his attention:

> "All thy garments smell of myrrh and aloes,
> and cassia, out of the ivory palaces
> whereby they have made thee glad."

"There," said Procter to himself, "is the name of our new soap—'Ivory.' " And a white soap became "Ivory Soap." The first bar of "Ivory" was sold in October, 1879.

An early "Ivory" advertisement in the *Century* for February, 1883, contained the phrase, "99-44/100 per cent pure," pictured a bar with the present standard appearance, and had testimonials of approval from the distinguished Benjamin Silliman, professor of chemistry at Yale, and H. B. Cornwall, who occupied a similar post at the College of New Jersey.

Procter and Gamble Company has never used "99-44/100 per cent pure" nor "It Floats" as technical slogans, but the phrases have become famous throughout the world. To this 99-44/100 per cent standard the company has remained steadfast and tells the world so in its advertising. "It Floats" means "Ivory Soap" and especially to those who recall the ghost stories built around

> "It floats.
> What floats?
> IVORY SOAP!"

MR. PEANUT

*Reproduced Courtesy Planters Nut and
Chocolate Company*

A NATIVE of Brazil, the peanut was carried by early
slave ships to Africa, when it was brought to this
country along with the slaves in colonial days. The
Civil War gave the first important impulse to its cul-
ture. Before then the peanut was little known outside
of Virginia, North Carolina, and Tennessee. When
the Union armies disbanded, the soldiers carried a
knowledge and an appreciation of peanuts to all parts
of the country.

The school children of a Virginia town played a
part in glorifying the peanut. In 1916, a contest was
launched among the school children of Suffolk to find
an appropriate trade-mark for Planters Nut and
Chocolate Company. The winning sketch was of

"Mr. Peanut" (lacking, however, the monocle and the negligently crooked leg, which were added by a commercial artist). The winner received five dollars and the sketch was the beginning of a famous trade-mark.

When you think of Planters you think of a symbol. The symbol is "Mr. Peanut," the long-legged, peanut-bodied character with the stove-pipe hat and the monocle. He is a thoroughly publicized personality. In gargantuan form he used to sit astride the peanut-bodied delivery trucks that salesmen formerly used. As a nine-foot embodied spirit he walks the streets of a hundred cities, making a show all himself and sometimes distributing samples. He also appears in other various unique forms of advertising.

The Planters Nut and Chocolate Company was organized in 1906 at Wilkes-Barre, Pennsylvania, by Mr. A. Obici and Mr. M. Peruzzi. Mr. Obici for several years had conducted a small peanut business and was known throughout the city of Wilkes-Barre as "the peanut specialist." The company was small at the beginning, but gradually their business grew. In 1912, a factory was established in the heart of the peanut country at Suffolk, Virginia. Five years later the company, with "Mr. Peanut," embarked on a large nation-wide advertising campaign, and the public acceptance of Planters' products increased rapidly in the years that followed. Today the Planters Nut and Chocolate Company is the world's largest dealer in peanut products, and "Mr. Peanut" one of the best-known trade-mark characters.

MONK'S FOOT

LEGEND HAS it that a monk, who placed bunches of live wool in his sandals to ease his tired feet, was the unconscious discoverer of felt.

In the days of Robert the Devil, a French monk, St. Feutre, in penance for his sins, started upon a pilgrimage to a distant shrine. The journey was tiresome and his feet were sore from his new sandals, and as he walked on he thought to himself that each step taken was a part of his penance. From time to time on his tedious journey he passed flocks of sheep and he wondered within his heart whether it would be displeasing to God if he should pluck a handful of wool from the backs of the sheep and put it in his sandals for his feet to tread upon. As he thus communed with himself it came to him that he would ask God to bless his action, so he plucked from the backs of the sheep several handfuls of wool which he placed upon the soles of his sandals, to his great comfort. As he pulled off his sandals at the end of his journey he found a new cloth, unknown before, firm of texture, soft to the touch and strong, made from the wool of the sheep, tramped down by the daily foot-steps of the pilgrim —felt.

In 1912, a great industrial organization, the American Felt Company, inspired by the legend, adopted a "Monk's Foot" as its trade-mark. This symbol is effective from the practical side also; the "Monk's Foot" is moving forward, making progress—it typifies a man or institution on its toes, progressing toward a goal.

The American Felt Company was incorporated in 1898. It has played a major part in making felt, "the material of a million uses."

JOHN B. STETSON

"STETSON" MEANS hat:

"If a man asks for a 'Stetson' in any civilized country in the world, the dealer knows what he wants."—*Elbert Hubbard.*

Even "John B" means hat:

"I'll bet you a 'John B' that Brown is elected to Congress." The taker of this wager knows that if Brown is defeated he wins a hat.

"Where did you get that 'John B'?" The question might be aimed at Al Smith's brown derby or a Texas Ranger's ten gallon western.

Seventy-six years ago, John B. Stetson, son of a Philadelphia hat maker, after spending several years in the West for his health, returned home long in experience and short in cash, and proceeded to set himself up in the hat business. The experience he had acquired in the West was not in making hats. He had become acquainted with the customs and needs of the farmer on the wind-swept prairies of the Middle West, the cowboy and cattleman of the plains, and the miner in the Pike's Peak region.

Mr. Stetson peddled a few hats patterned on the hats in vogue at that time around Philadelphia without much success. He even created new styles, but the dealers informed him that styles came from Paris and London and not Philadelphia. Then one day his Western experience began to assert itself. Instead of depending upon local trade and haggling with dealers as to price, Stetson decided to make a big, fine, picturesque hat for the Cattle Kings and call it "The Boss of the Plains." Samples of his "Mexican sombrero with a college education" were sent to hat dealers in the Southwest, and orders came in rapidly. The hat became immensely popular, and Stetson's business from then on became only a question of his ability to fill orders.

In 1891, Stetson incorporated his business under the name of John B. Stetson Company, and at the present time there are perhaps more hats sold under the Stetson name and trade-mark than any other brand in the world. A few years ago the company adopted the slogan, "Step Out With A Stetson."

AUNT JEMIMA

Reproduced Courtesy of The Quaker Oats Company

ACCORDING TO an old legend Aunt Jemima was a mammy cook, famous throughout the length and breadth of the Old South in those golden days "befo' de Wah." Her master was Colonel Higbee, owner of a vast plantation at Higbee's Landing on the Mississippi River. The Colonel's hospitality was famous even in that universally hospitable era—famous because of his qualities as a host and famous because of Aunt Jemima's cooking. Her pancakes, made from a secret recipe, were the envy of many a Southern cook.

In 1886, Aunt Jemima sold her recipe for pancakes to the R. T. Davis Mill Company, of St. Joseph, Missouri. She appeared in person in an exhibit at the Chicago World's Fair in 1893, featuring "Aunt Jemima" Pancake Flour.

Although first registered in 1903, "Aunt Jemima" has been used as a trade-mark since 1889. In 1925, the Aunt Jemima Mills Company, of St. Joseph, Missouri, assigned the trade-mark to The Quaker Oats Company.

The "Aunt Jemima" trade-mark has been extended to include cooking and salad oils, dolls, candy, grits, etc., and the present owner has maintained "Aunt Jemima's" popularity by keeping her constantly before the public.

WE FIND reference to the pen in the Bible; Shakespeare wrote with a goose quill; Lincoln signed the Emancipation Proclamation with a steel pen; but it was left for Waterman to perfect the fountain pen.

The trade-mark "Waterman's" has been associated with the fountain pen for over half a century. It was taken from the name of the inventor of the modern fountain pen and the founder of L. E. Waterman Company. How Mr. Waterman came to perfect the fountain pen is an interesting anecdote. The inventor was at one time an insurance agent, and he carried one of those early fountain pens as a "business help." One day, when he was soliciting insurance, a prominent contractor agreed to sign up with him for a large policy. The appointment was made. Waterman expected to secure a large commission on his successful salesmanship. The time came and the contractor happened to be up-town at the site of a large building operation. Mr. Waterman appeared, and found his man. He pulled out his application and handed the prospect his fountain pen to sign. The pen leaked and the ink ran over the lower half of the application. It would have to be rewritten—but it was not, because a rival insurance man, before this was done, signed up the contractor. Waterman thus came to realize the need of a real fountain pen in the business world and he made one for himself. Then he made a few by hand for his friends. Next he opened a little shop, back of a cigar store on Fulton Street, New York. Then he was making two hundred pens in a year, all by hand. Last year more than two million were sold.

While "Waterman's" is the company's principal trade-mark today, it still extensively uses the old and well known trade-mark, "Ideal." The word "Ideal," the first trade-mark used in connection with a fountain pen, was chosen because the name appealed to the inventor, Mr. Lewis E. Waterman. As a matter of fact, his first company was called the Ideal Pen Company.

While the present company, L. E. Waterman Company, was not incorporated until 1887 the business really started in 1884 when Mr. Waterman was granted his first patent.

The fame and extent of business of the "Waterman's" pen is perhaps best described by the phrase which accompanies the "Ideal" trade-mark—"Makes Its Mark Around The World."

THE BEER THAT MADE MILWAUKEE
FAMOUS

THE SLOGAN, "The Beer That Made Milwaukee Famous," has been used with Schlitz Beer for a long time. A label carrying the phrase was registered in 1895. Just who at the brewery said it first, or in what piece of advertising it was first used, or who was responsible for its adoption cannot be ascertained by available facts—the expression must have "just growed" like Topsy.

The words in the phrase are literally true. Mention Milwaukee almost anywhere and somebody present knows that it is the home of "The Beer That Made Milwaukee Famous." It has contributed materially to the advertisement of its home town.

The owners of the slogan, Jos. Schlitz Brewing Company, have consistently used it in their advertising, on their bottles, containers, delivery trucks, etc. No trade phrase is more closely associated with a product than "The Beer That Made Milwaukee Famous."

BENJAMIN FRANKLIN HEAD

Reg. U. S. Pat. Off.
*Reproduced Courtesy of The Curtis
Publishing Company*

THE "BENJAMIN Franklin Head" trade-mark appears on the masthead of the world's greatest weekly magazine in prestige and circulation—THE SATURDAY EVENING POST. When Cyrus H. K. Curtis purchased the magazine in 1897 it was dead for all intents and purposes. It was worth the $1,000 he paid for it only for the Benjamin Franklin tradition.

The present magazine is the lineal descendant of *The Universal Instructor in All Arts and Sciences and Pennsylvania Gazette,* first published in Philadelphia on the day before Christmas in the year 1728. The paper was conceived by Benjamin Franklin when he was twenty-two years of age. He talked over his idea with a man named Webb, a printer recently released from indenture by Samuel Keimer, once Franklin's employer, too. Franklin promised Webb a job "in a matter of five or six days, when we commence work on our newspaper"; but Webb went directly to Keimer, repeated all that Franklin had said, and the better equipped Keimer launched the weekly before Franklin could act. It was not a success, and after a few months Franklin bought it for a nominal sum, dropping the bombastic first part of the title. *The Pennsylvania Gazette* issued from the press of B. Franklin, printer, October 2, 1729. In a short time it became the best known paper in the Colonies.

In the years that followed, name and ownership changed several times, and the paper had its ups and downs. Nearly a century after its founding, it was rechristened THE SATURDAY EVENING POST, and was on its last legs when purchased by Mr. Curtis. Under the leadership of the late George Horace Lorimer (editor 1899-1937) THE SATURDAY EVENING POST became an American institution. Today it has over 3,000,000 buyers weekly.

From the beginning of Mr. Lorimer's editorship he strongly emphasized the publication's descent from Franklin, but the original trade-mark was not registered until 1911. The present "Benjamin Franklin Head" emblem was designed and registered in the year 1929, the two-hundredth anniversary of *The Pennsylvania Gazette,* the publication founded by Benjamin Franklin.

MUNSINGWEAR

Reg. U. S. Pat. Off.
Reproduced Courtesy of Munsingwear, Inc.

"MUNSINGWEAR" IS derived from the name of the inventor of the union suit, Mr. George D. Munsing.

In 1886, Mr. Munsing left the East with two young men, graduates of Massachusetts Institute of Technology, and formed a partnership, The Northwestern Knitting Company, at Minneapolis, to knit underwear. Not only had Mr. Munsing invented the union suit, he had also developed a method in knitting which provided warmth without irritation to the skin from contact with worsted yarns.

On March 1, 1887, the partnership was incorporated and the new company started labeling its goods "The Munsing." The name was registered as a trademark in 1906. The "wear" was added to the name "Munsing" in 1911. This action was taken so that the trade-mark would be a little more distinctive and also indicate that it applied to wearing apparel. In 1920, the name of The Northwestern Knitting Company was changed to The Munsingwear Corporation (now Munsingwear, Inc.).

Anticipating an export business, the company, in 1922, decided to register its trade-mark in foreign countries. In order to make the trade-mark more distinctive, a shield was added under the letter "U"

65

bearing "cupped and fretted" chevrons. The company by this time was prominent in the underwear business, and was not content with the ordinary inverted V form of chevron used by the army to denote the rank of corporal or sergeant. A much higher rank was desired. In searching the documents of a public library a reproduction of a shield with "cupped and fretted" chevrons as carried by a titled Englishman in one of the first Crusades, was discovered. This seemed to fill the bill and it was adopted. Today, "Munsingwear," with its chevrons, represents a high rank of leadership in the wearing apparel industry.

In 1869, the two oceans bounding the United States were linked by the first trans-continental railroad. A young Yankee from Maine had been doing a little trans-continental thinking himself. In that year he changed the name of his business from "The Great American Tea Company" to "The Great Atlantic and Pacific Tea Company" and proceeded on a coast-to-coast expansion to match the achievements of the Union Pacific. The Yankee was Mr. George Huntington Hartford, founder of the "A & P" food stores, and his business at that time consisted of thirty or forty red-fronted tea and coffee stores in and around New York City.

Mr. Hartford's No. 1 store was opened on Vesey Street in New York City in 1859. The store, which sold only tea and coffee, did well from the start. Before the close of the year two more such stores were added, and the chain began. By the early seventies he had stores in nearly all of the principal cities in the United States. Wagons were sent over the country-side offering his products for sale in the rural communities. He gradually added other lines to his business, such as extracts, rice, soap, etc., but it was not until the close of the century that he operated a chain of full-fledged grocery stores. By 1912, he had approximately four hundred "A & P" stores scattered throughout the country selling a general line of groceries.

The founder of the great enterprise died in 1917, but his two sons, who had grown up in the business from boyhood, have carried on. They are John A. Hartford, now president of the company, and George L. Hartford, the present chairman of the board of directors.

From 1912 to 1930, "A & P" stores leaped from four hundred to nearly sixteen thousand. Such a rapid expansion never has been known in business history. Today The Great Atlantic and Pacific Tea Company is one of America's largest industrial organizations. In fact, you can count on your fingers the companies that do a comparable gross business.

The name, "The Great Atlantic and Pacific Tea Company," which was chosen seventy-two years ago, sounds rather ambitious and pretentious, based on today's standards of enterprise, as the name for a few tea and coffee stores operating solely in the New York City area. But the late sixties were days of expansion —our frontier was moving westward, and those with vision were rewarded by seeing their dreams materialize. The country is now dotted with the red-front stores from the Atlantic to the Pacific.

Reg. U. S. Pat. Off.
*Reproduced Courtesy of The United States Playing
Card Company*

THE NAME, "Bicycle," for playing cards originated in 1885, in consequence of a desire to meet the competition of another brand of playing cards known as "Tally-Ho," which was very prominent at that time. The word, "Tally-Ho," of course, suggested an out-of-door sporting atmosphere, but also implied wealth, as the tallyho, with its expensive horses and footmen, was not the vehicle of the general public. The idea at the time was for something parallel to "Tally-Ho" and also connected with out-of-door sporting life, but which would have a much more general appeal. For these reasons "Bicycle" was suggested.

At that time, the bicycle in use was the old-fashioned high-wheel type which was quite dangerous on account of the height from which the rider fell in case of an accident. For this reason, perhaps, "Bicycle" did not become so popular a brand until the advent of the safety bicycle with its smaller wheels some five years later, at which time the sales greatly increased.

In 1893, a reproduction of a safety bicycle was registered as a trade-mark. The word, "Bicycle," had been registered previously. The famous Joker, as illustrated, depicting the king out of a deck of cards riding a bicycle, is also a trade-mark. On the back of the Joker are pictures of riders mounted on the old-fashioned high-wheel bicycles.

A picture of a bicycle has always appeared on the backs of the cards produced by The United States Playing Card Company; and while the popularity of the bicycle has varied throughout the years, the "Bicycle" playing cards, once firmly established, have remained constantly popular.

GILLETTE

Reg. U. S. Pat. Off.
Reproduced Courtesy of Gillette Safety Razor Company

OF ALL the little things that have been invented, the safety razor is perhaps the biggest little thing that ever has been patented. The inventor was King C. Gillette.

Mr. Gillette, from boyhood, displayed an inventive turn of mind. The idea of inventing something that could be used and thrown away was planted in his mind when he was a salesman for the Baltimore Seal Company (later Crown Cork & Seal Company) and became intimately acquainted with William Painter, the inventor of the Crown Cork. In an article written by Mr. Gillette in 1925 on the origin of the Gillette razor he quotes the advice given him by Mr. Painter, which he says he never forgot: "King, you are always thinking and inventing something; why don't you try to think of something like the Crown Cork which, when once used, is thrown away? And the customer keeps coming back for more—and with every additional customer you get, you are building a permanent foundation of profit."

In 1895, when shaving with a dull razor of the type then in vogue, Mr. Gillette received his first inspiration of a razor with separate blades. After half-a-dozen years of research and experimental work, he invented the Gillette safety razor which is today basically the same as his original model.

A diamond shaped trade-mark, as illustrated, was selected as the Gillette trade-mark in 1906 and it is used on the company's products and in its advertising. The picture of the inventor, King C. Gillette, is also frequently used.

The Gillette Safety Razor Company has factories in several foreign countries and sales agencies in every country in the world. Its products may be found in dealers' stocks ranging from the bazaar merchants of India and the army quartermaster canteens, deep in the jungles of distant lands, to the smartest shops on Fifth Avenue, New York

WHEN IT RAINS IT POURS

Reg. U. S. Pat. Off.
Reproduced Courtesy of Morton Salt Company

MANY A nationally known slogan could apply to products in different fields, but none could be more apropos of salt than the slogan "When It Rains It Pours." The housewife in damp weather knows and appreciates the significance of this phrase.

The origin of the slogan was in 1911. In that year the Morton Salt Company placed on the market a new grade of table salt which ran freely from salt shakers. In a small booklet describing the product and package, a copy writer used as a paragraph heading the words, "When It Rains It Pours," a revision of the old saying, "It Never Rains But It Pours." A paragraph heading thus became an effective slogan.

About the same time an artist submitted to the Morton Salt Company a painting of his little daughter under an umbrella with a package of salt under her arm which seemed to fit with the slogan and the little girl was adopted as a trade-mark.

COMMUNITY PLATE

THE TRADE-MARK, "Community Plate," has a very unusual history which began nearly a hundred years ago. Oneida, Ltd. (formerly Oneida Community, Limited), the present owner of this trade-mark, is an institutional descendant of the original Oneida Community.

In 1848, at Oneida, New York, under the leadership of John Humphrey Noyes, there was established a group of three hundred people who called themselves the "Oneida Community." It was a Christian Communistic organization. For more than thirty years they lived together in one great building, the "Mansion House," sharing everything in common, dispensing entirely with conventional love and marriage, and bringing into the world a group of eugenically selected children whom they reared and educated jointly away from their parents. These people were idealistic, peace-loving, and industrious.

At first the ambitions of the Communists were simple. They hoped to support themselves by agriculture and horticulture; but, in a few years, finding their capital depleted, their leader urged that business be made a part of their religion, and industrial enterprises were started. They first experimented with the canning of their crops for sale to grocers. It was a successful venture and for more than seventy years "Community Fruits and Vegetables" enjoyed a high reputation throughout the United States. The manufacture of steel traps was another success. Professional trappers would take no other brand. For over half a century all the traps used by the Hudson Bay Company were made at Oneida. A silk factory was established, and "Community Silk" thread became well and favorably known. In 1877, the Wallingford, Connecticut, branch of the Community was provided with an industry all its own—the making of tablewear. It is said that when the Community was preparing to enter this field, the leading manufacturer of silver-plated tableware showed his fear of Communistic competition by offering to buy the entire output of the Community factory.

In 1880, due to internal strife and outside criticism, the Oneida Community was dissolved and a corporation was formed, Oneida Community, Limited, to take over the different businesses, the members of the Community being the stockholders.

The silver-plated tableware enterprise at Wallingford was not particularly successful until the introduction of a heavy high grade of silver-plate in 1901. This new silver-plate ware was designated "Community" silver and registered as a trade-mark in 1907. It established a new standard for high grade silver-plate and became very popular. The name was changed later to "Community Plate." This name had been used in Canada because it was unlawful there to use the word "silver" on any article which was not solid silver, and anticipating the United States would pass a similar law, the name was changed here.

It is interesting to note that the man who is responsible for the present high standard of "Community Plate" is now president of the company—Mr. Pierrepont B. Noyes, son of the founder of the original Community at Oneida. He still lives in the old "Mansion House" where he was born.

KEEN KUTTER

"KEEN KUTTER" has been the trade-mark, for seventy-one years, of Simmons Hardware Company, which was formed in the sixties.

To the American boy, "Keen Kutter" means a jack-knife; to the old codger, whittling by the stove in the village store, as well as to the wood cutter of yesterday and today, this name is familiar.

In 1870, Mr. E. C. Simmons, the founder of the Simmons Hardware Company, was placing his order for axes for the fall. He told the manufacturer, for whom his company had been distributing axes in the Middle West for a few years, that his company would require a better price or else they would build an axe under their own private brand. The manufacturer refused his request, so Mr. Simmons that same day started whittling out of soft pine the design of an axe which he thought would meet the requirements of every purchaser. It took him until three o'clock in the morning to complete the job to his liking, and when it was finished he was so pleased with it that when he looked at it, he said to himself, "We'll call you the Simmons 'Keen Kutter.'" It came as an inspiration and while it was applied only to axes at first, the name became so popular that following its copyright that same year, it was used with other tools, particularly those having cutting edges, and today "Keen Kutter" is an outstanding brand in the hardware field.

COVER THE EARTH

Reproduced Courtesy of The Sherwin-Williams Co.

THE ORIGINAL trade-mark of The Sherwin-Williams Co., was an oval painter's palette, around the edge of which was coiled a Chameleon. This was designed by the founders of the company and was widely used for many years.

In the early nineties, in Cleveland, Ohio, Mr. George W. Ford, then advertising manager of The Sherwin-Williams Co., was also interested in a small concern which manufactured a cleaning compound known as "Eureka." This Eureka cleaner was designed for general use, and one day Mr. Ford, in considering some advertising material, made a rough sketch of the globe, with the map of the world, and small Brownies climbing over it with packages of Eureka Cleaner in one hand, and scrubbing brushes in the other—cleaning the world.

This was the germ of the idea from which the now famous "Cover the Earth" trade-mark of Sherwin-

Williams was born. The Eureka concern went out of existence after a few months. In 1893, when Sherwin-Williams began expanding, Mr. Ford, hunting for an idea that would convey this expansion thought, remembered his old Eureka drawing. He remade it, showing a can of paint pouring over the earth. The design first made its commercial appearance in Massachusetts. The idea was accepted at once, and "Cover the Earth" was used on the company's merchandise and featured in their advertising constantly from that time on. In 1895, it was officially adopted as the Sherwin-Williams trade-mark, supplanting the old Chameleon.

The emblem has been slightly refined, in order to simplify reproduction, but the original idea has been unchanged. Today it appears on every package of Sherwin-Williams merchandise and is a well-recognized outdoor billboard in those commercial locations where outdoor advertising has its place. The trade-mark may not literally cover the earth, but it is seen in nearly every country of the world.

PALM BEACH

PALM BEACH has two meanings in the minds of most people—a winter resort in Florida, and cool clothing for warm weather. The "Beach" part of the clothing name, however, originated in Maine, not Florida.

In the latter part of 1905, William S. Nutter, a recognized expert in the production of textile fabrics, invented a cloth suitable for wearing apparel in warm weather. In search of a name for his product, Mr. Nutter, while walking along the beach near his home in Maine, conceived the name "Beach Cloth" for a trade-mark.

Prior to this time, the business of light-weight suits was negligible and unprofitable, but with the advent of this new textile fabric, it grew by leaps and bounds. In January, 1909, the trade-mark, "Beach Cloth," was changed to "Palm Beach," probably because of the increasing popularity of the Florida winter resort of that name.

The fame of "Palm Beach" is now international, and has become a synonym for Goodall Worsted Company, the manufacturers and sellers of the product.

TIME TO RE-TIRE
"GET A FISK"

Reg. U. S. Pat. Off.
Reproduced Courtesy of United States Rubber Company

EVERYWHERE THE name Fisk appears, the little night-robed boy stands as mascot. He is known all over the world and registered in more than ninety countries.

In 1907, an eighteen-year-old artist, Burr Giffen, showed an official of the Fisk Rubber Company a rough pencil sketch, colored with ordinary crayons, which he had designed depicting a yawning child in a one-piece pajama suit with a tire over his shoulder and a candle in his hand. The picture was the artist's conception of a trade-mark for the Fisk Rubber Company. The slogan with the picture read, "When It's Time to Re-tire, Buy a Fisk." The idea appealed to the management and the sketch was purchased and adopted as the official trade-mark. Eleven years later another artist, Mr. Edward M. Eggleston, was commissioned to make an oil painting of Mr. Giffen's sketch.

In 1928, the picture of the yawning boy was changed to a happy, smiling boy. Two years later, Fisk announced a tire built on a new principle and the company decided to modernize the boy to keep pace with its new product, so, in 1930, a happy, smiling boy in his two-piece pajamas, radiating good cheer, and standing in the old-time pose but with a new model tire over his shoulder greeted the world. Shortly after this change, the company went into receivership and advertising was virtually suspended for six years.

In 1936, a new management came into the company and one of the first things done was to return to the original trade-mark of the yawning boy in his first costume.

Again an old adage, paraphrased, disclosed its wisdom: "Change the product, change the package, change the advertising, but *touch not a line on yon gray trade-mark.*"

On January 1, 1940, the United States Rubber Company purchased the Fisk Rubber Company. The painting of the trade-mark by Mr. Eggleston was restored to its original appearance, as illustrated. It not only represents the design that is so well known over the world, but is the one that will be used hereafter as the Fisk trade-mark.

THERE'S A REASON!

WEARY, ILL, and discouraged at thirty-six, Charles William Post left his home and farm-tool business in Illinois in the early nineties to seek a return to health in a Battle Creek, Michigan, sanitarium. When the health center's routine treatments failed to produce in his condition the results he anticipated, he took up the study of foods and their relation to health.

Research produced ideas, and ideas led to experiments. In a barn he set up a coffee grinder, a gasoline stove, and other crude equipment. From a few dollars worth of wheat, bran, and molasses, and much labor, there emerged a new food beverage—Postum.

In a horse and buggy he visited store after store, demonstrating and explaining the merits of his new product. And to all he would say, "There's a reason!" He advertised and the public responded. "There's a Reason!" became a popular saying and the name, Postum, grew into a household word. Today it is the mealtime drink in millions of homes.

Other products followed. Spic-and-span factories mushroomed at Battle Creek to meet the demand for products with the "C. W. Post" trade-mark. Grape-Nuts, one of the first packaged, ready-to-serve cereals, was introduced in 1897. Seven years later the Post organization entered the corn flakes field with Post Toasties.

Mr. Post died in 1914, but the original organization

which he had founded continued to grow. In 1922, the company was reorganized under the name of Postum Cereal Company, Inc., which was later changed to Postum Company, Inc., and, in 1929, became General Foods Corporation.

DUTCH BOY

INASMUCH AS the Dutch were the first to manufacture white lead by a commercially practicable process known as the Old Dutch Process, it was fitting that the National Lead Company should adopt as their emblem the "Dutch Boy Painter." This trade-mark was registered in 1907.

Rudolph Yook, of George Batten Company, a New York advertising agency, made a few pencil drawings, for the National Lead Company, of a Dutch boy dressed in painter's overalls in the act of painting. These drawings were made solely for advertising illustrations. A little later, when the company was considering a trade-mark, the president, Mr. L. A. Cole, now deceased, remarked, "Would not one of those Dutch boys you showed me some time ago make a good trade-mark?" The suggestion was acted upon at once; one of the sketches was selected, re-drawn, and adopted. Mr. Lawrence Carmichael

Earle, a well-known artist, who had spent several years in Holland studying art, was commissioned to put the rough sketch into a permanent painting.

The National Lead Company was incorporated in 1891, although some of the companies which went into its makeup date back to Colonial times. At the time the "Dutch Boy" trade-mark was created, the National Lead Company marketed about twenty different brands of white-lead-in-oil, each brand selling in a different section of the country. The local brands were retained when the "Dutch Boy" trade-mark was adopted. The mark was simply superimposed upon the old brands. In this way all the brands were brought together in a common family relationship, while, at the same time, the prestige of each local brand was retained.

When the "Dutch Boy" was first used as a trade-mark it appeared only on white-lead-in-oil; later its use was extended to red-lead, linseed oil, and other paint materials which the National Lead Company now manufactures, and finally to such metal products as solder, babbit metal, and lead pipe.

The "Dutch Boy" emblem is well known for its commercial significance and is one of America's familiar trade-mark characters. The original canvas, which is a work of art, now hangs in the office of the president of the company.

LOUISVILLE SLUGGER

NINETEEN THIRTY-NINE was baseball's one hundredth anniversary and the event was celebrated from sand lot to major league. No article was more universally used that year by baseball players than the "Louisville Slugger."

Fifty-five years ago, Pete Browning, a heavy hitter on the Louisville baseball team, stepped into a little wood-trimming shop in Louisville and asked the proprietor, Mr. J. A. Hillerich, if he could make a bat for him according to his own specifications. Mr. Hillerich told Pete that he thought he could. After selecting a piece of suitable wood they proceeded to turn it into a bat. Every now and then Pete would take the bludgeon, swing it, look it over, and then give additional instructions. Finally Pete pronounced the bat satisfactory. After playing with it for some time he ordered another one made with the same specifications, and his results with these bats were so outstanding that other players came to Mr. Hillerich to have their bats custom made. Requests grew so rapidly that a few years later Mr. Hillerich abandoned his wood trimming shop and started manufacturing "Louisville Sluggers." This name was registered as a trade-mark in 1893 but probably was used as early as 1887.

For half a century the "Louisville Slugger" has been the leading bat used by amateurs and professionals. It was the choice of Ty Cobb, Hans Wagner, and Babe Ruth. In fact, it is estimated that it has been used by 95 per cent of the famous sluggers of the national game. No doubt a check up would disclose the bat was used by "Our Gang" of the movies.

Hillerich and Bradsby Company are the owners of the trade-mark and are now manufacturing "Louisville Sluggers" at Louisville, Kentucky.

THE SHELL

MANY PEOPLE have wondered how the Shell Oil Company, with all its ramifications, nationally and internationally, dealing in petroleum products, happened to choose the "Shell" as its emblem.

The story of "Shell" opens in a little shop of a curio dealer in London during the last century. One summer day the children of this curio dealer left for a holiday at the seashore, taking with them a small box of lunch. While romping on the beach they found their first seashells, and later, their lunch gone, they amused themselves by fastening their new playthings to the empty box. When they proudly displayed their handiwork at home, their father saw that the idea might catch the fancy of his customers. He began to manufacture shell-covered souvenir boxes, labeling them as gifts from one or another well-known resort. Soon the boxes were selling in stores all along the sea-coast. His little shop grew until his line of goods in-cluded shells from distant lands and his name became identified with conchology. A company was formed which was later to build up a large international trade in mother-of-pearl, oriental curios, and copra. Bar-reled kerosene next appeared in the firm's cargo lists. Once launched in the kerosene trade, the world-wide trading activities of this small London curio dealer were carried on under the name of the Shell Trading and Transport Company and they expanded rapidly into a great oil company. Today that company, deal-ing exclusively in oil products, still bears the name of "Shell" and still uses as its emblem the graceful sea-shell admired by the founder's children. Thus it was that the "Shell" emblem—and all that it now stands for—had its birth in the mind of one man who saw the worth of an idea.

The "Shell" is now a universal stop signal for oil products for motorists almost everywhere.

LIFE SAVERS

"LIFE SAVERS" is the name of a ring-shaped candy with a hole in it produced in various flavors and there is, perhaps, no product on the market today which has more retail outlets. It is estimated that there are seven places where they can be purchased in every block of a city business district.

In 1912, Clarence A. Crane, manufacturer of Crane's & Mary Garden Chocolates in Cleveland, Ohio, decided to add a line of hard mints to boost his summer business. Mr. Crane made his mints in the shape of a ring in order to distinguish them from the square German and Austrian mints which were being sold in this country, and called them "Life Savers." Obviously, this name was suggested from their miniature likeness to a ship's life saver.

After "Life Savers" had been on the market for about a year Mr. Crane sold his stock and trade-mark to two young men, Edward J. Noble and J. Roy Allen. In the early days, "Life Savers" were a "drug on the market," but under the leadership of Mr. Noble and Mr. Allen, they rose to fame. These clever merchandisers have never lost sight of the advertising value of the likeness of their product to a ship's life saver, and they continually emphasize the nautical idea in their publicity. Millions of sample packages are given away each year by girl distributors dressed in attractive blue and white sailor suits.

The trade name, "Life Savers," is now the property of Life Savers Corporation, of Port Chester, New York.

CELLOPHANE

To THE purchasing public the trade-mark, "Cellophane," suggests an unusual wrapping material of absolute transparency. Two decades ago very few people of this country ever heard of the word or the product. Its public acceptance is another du Pont achievement.

The validity of "Cellophane" as a trade-mark is now in litigation. There is no question, however, as to who originated the name, or as to who made the product popular.

The name is fanciful. It was coined by Mr. Brandenberger, of Bezans, France, in 1909, as suggesting a transparent product made of cellulose, and registered "La Cellophane," written in fancy script as a trade-mark. A French company began selling "Cellophane" through an agent in this country in 1912. The product was never extensively sold here, however, until a national advertising campaign was started in 1927, a few years after the du Pont interests had acquired the North American rights to "Cellophane" from the French company.

The business, now operated by E. I. du Pont de Nemours & Company, was established in 1802. The name du Pont has been identified with a large diversity of products, and has been a valuable trade-mark for many years. When "Cellophane" appeared on the market associated with the famous du Pont oval trade-mark, the public at once accepted it, as it has for many years accepted other du Pont products.

Today "Cellophane" is the best known means of keeping merchandise protected and yet completely visible.

CREAM OF WHEAT

Reg. U. S. Pat. Off.
*Reproduced Courtesy of The Cream of Wheat
Corporation*

WHEN MR. Tom Amidon began making "Cream of Wheat" in a small flour mill at Grand Forks, North Dakota, in 1895, he established a new technique in grocery merchandising by introducing food packaging. The trade-mark, "Cream of Wheat," was coined but there is no record as to whose imagination supplied the name.

The story of "Rastus," the negro chef, whose picture appears in the advertising and on the cartons with the words, "Cream of Wheat," is better known. A crude picture of a negro chef was used on the label when "Cream of Wheat" made its first appearance on the market. The picture came from a miscellaneous lot of printing material owned by one of the officers of the Milling Company, who had been formerly in the printing business. This original label was used for about ten years, but the executives of the company were never entirely satisfied with the picture of the chef. Then one day, Mr. Emery Mapes, a company officer at that time, while having breakfast at Kohlsaat's restaurant in Chicago, saw there a handsome negro waiter. The idea immediately struck him that a picture of this negro waiter would be a better display on the label than the crude picture then being used. For the sum of five dollars the negro agreed to be photographed, and since that time his face has appeared as the well-known "Cream of Wheat Chef." From the day the photograph was taken, no one in the Cream of Wheat organization has come in contact with this negro waiter. Many have represented themselves as being the original "Rastus," but the imposters have been detected.

"Cream of Wheat," which appears so frequently on many breakfast tables, is now manufactured by The Cream of Wheat Corporation, of Minneapolis, Minnesota.

VASELINE

IT IS a rather odd fact that the medicinal qualities of petroleum were discovered before the discovery of the substance itself. As we know, oil was not really "discovered" until the sinking of the first well by Colonel Edwin L. Drake, near Titusville, Pennsylvania, in 1859, and it was from that time only that the development of oil, for its scores of uses, dated. For hundreds of years before Drake, oil was found in many parts of the world, and at first almost the only use of these widely scattered seepages was medicinal. For example, late in the thirteenth century the explorer, Marco Polo, in traveling through Baku, found they were using petroleum oil for treatment of diseased camels.

The Chesebrough Manufacturing Company was among the pioneer manufacturers of oil products, making kerosene oil, and selling it under the trademark "Luxor" oil, and other products. Mr. Robert A. Chesebrough, one of the firm, believed that it was possible by different refining methods to retain the medicinal qualities of the oil; and he devoted much time to experimenting in his company's laboratories. Through refining exclusively by heat and confining his cleaning processes to filtering, he finally produced the first Petroleum Jelly. He knew he had a new therapeutic substance and proved by further experiment its healing and curative properties. He gave his product the name "Vaseline," which he coined.

Mr. Chesebrough first submitted his product to scientific and medical societies, and it received favorable comments and awards. *The London Lancet,* then and now possibly the leading medical journal of the world, gave it notice on May 13, 1876, part of which was, "It is very soft and altogether seems admirably adapted to the purpose for which it is intended. We think it will be very valuable for medicinal practice and advise its careful trial." Doctors throughout Europe and America began using "Vaseline." Soon Mr. Chesebrough decided not to confine his product to the medical and pharmaceutical fraternity, and started to advertise it generally. The purchasing public responded, and today "Vaseline" is a registered trade-mark throughout the world and can be purchased nearly everywhere.

FOUR ROSES

IF SPACE permitted, stories behind many of the well-known old American whiskies would be included.

The origins of some of the famous brands date back many years. Old Oscar Pepper, for instance, has been known to connoisseurs since 1838. A list of Who's Who in Bourbons and Ryes would include Four Roses, Old Taylor, Green River, Old Crow, Paul Jones, Old Grand-Dad, Old Oscar Pepper, Mount Vernon, Golden Wedding, Old Overholt, and Hunter's Baltimore Rye.

"Four Roses" is now, and has been for many years, one of the most popular brands, and here is the story of the origin of the name: In the spring of 1865, a Confederate officer, Colonel Paul Jones, turned homeward from the battlefields. His family fortune was gone, lost with the cause he fought for.

In the Southland he established a still. Before long the whisky he made had won an honored place on the sideboards of the nation. Its name, like the name of its maker, was Paul Jones. Years later a descendant of Colonel Paul Jones decided to bring forth another brand of whisky, and he remembered a story —how in the days before the Civil War a lovely lady

had signified her acceptance of the Colonel's court-
ship by wearing to a cotillion a corsage of four red
roses, and so "Four Roses" came into being.

The Frankfort Distilleries, Incorporated, which
now makes "Four Roses," is owned and operated by
the descendants of the old Colonel. The trade-mark
"Four Roses" has been used by the present company
and its predecessors since 1888.

ARROW

THE "ARROW" trade-mark was conceived by Albert Coon, a son of J. H. Coon, one of the partners of Coon & Co. (which later consolidated with George B. Cluett Bros. & Co.), in 1885. Just before it was announced to the trade, the following riddle was published in various trade journals:

> "I'm narrow, I'm long,
>   I'm fast, an' I'm slow,
> I'm young an' I'm old
>   An' I fly from a beau
> 'Fore powder was made
>   My feathers were gray,
> But my youth is renewed
>   From day unto day."

A short time later the name was announced and "Arrow" collars manufactured by Coon & Co., made their initial appearance in the world.

The name "Arrow" grew in popularity. Letters from dealers and customers arrived simply addressed "The Arrow Collar Company." The owners of the popular name saw the advantage in applying it to ties, shirts, and other articles they produced.

If today, Cluett, Peabody & Company were to make a pre-announcement merely using the trade-mark, "Arrow," (instead of a riddle contest used fifty-six years ago) the public would know what to expect.

Reg. U. S. Pat. Off.
*Reproduced Courtesy of Colt's Patent Fire Arms
Manufacturing Company*

OUR "G MEN" carry it; so do village constables; it has been used by the Texas Rangers, Kit Carson, and the mountain men, as well as the Forty-niners. It became a business success when General Zachary Taylor ordered one thousand in 1847 for his army in Mexico. It has been used in all our wars since that time. Such is the record of the "Colt" revolver.

As a Yankee youngster of fourteen, on board a sailing ship bound for Calcutta, Samuel Colt completed a working model of what was to be a revolver. In 1835, having perfected a six-barreled rotating breech, he patented his invention in London and Paris. The next year it was patented in this country and a small factory was established at Paterson, New Jersey, for the manufacture of the first "Colt" revolvers. The factory was moved several times and the business did not prosper until the order came from General Taylor.

The emblem of the little colt, indicative of the name of the inventor, Mr. Samuel Colt, appears on the revolver as well as on other products of the company. Apparently, it was used first in its present form about 1865. There is a tradition that it was preceded by the representation of a running horse or colt (as contrasted with the rampant colt), having an unbroken spear in its mouth. This running horse trademark may have been used by the present company's predecessor for the guns manufactured in the late eighteen-thirties.

The present trade-mark, consisting of a rampant colt with the broken spear, is commonly understood to be based on the legend of a knight who was killed in action, his spear being broken as he fell from the horse. The horse picked up the broken spear and continued the combat.

A little armory in Connecticut, where the order for Mexico was executed, became, in time, an enormous factory of the Colt's Patent Fire Arms Manufacturing Company. During the hundred years that the "Colt" has been on the market, many improvements have been made to enhance its efficiency and accuracy.

P. K.

To the purchasing public, Wrigley and chewing gum are nearly synonymous. This conclusion is not surprising when one realizes that the name Wrigley has been connected with the sale of chewing gum for almost fifty years, and that the Wm. Wrigley Jr. Company for many years has been one of the largest advertisers in the world.

But where did the trade-mark "P. K." come from and why? At the beginning of 1921 the Wm. Wrigley Jr. Company decided to again introduce a sugar-coated gum. Every good name suggested for the product seemed to conflict with other names already on the market. Somewhat in desperation the late William Wrigley, Jr., exclaimed, "Why not call it P-Ks?" These are the initials of his son, P. K. Wrigley, who is now president of the existing company. A competitor, who put out a product called "Peaks," objected to the trade-mark "P-Ks," and the Wrigley Company changed it to "P. K." and registered it in April, 1923.

It was thought that registration of this trade-mark in some foreign countries might be troublesome because of the fact that "K" does not exist in the French and Spanish languages. However, no serious difficulty was encountered.

WHO'S YOUR TAILOR?

Reg. U. S. Pat. Off.
Reproduced Courtesy of Ed. V. Price & Co.

THE "JOLLY Little Tailor," coupled with the slogan "Who's Your Tailor?" is known in nearly every city, town, and hamlet in the United States, and in fact, to a large extent all over the world.

In 1895, Mr. Ed. V. Price started in a relatively small way a merchant tailoring service in Chicago through dealers by mail, which was a comparatively new idea of merchandising at that time. It filled a real need and his business flourished. Shortly after he launched this tailoring service an artist suggested as a slogan the use of an owl and the words, "Who's Your Tailor?" Some years later Mr. Price dropped the owl and copyrighted "Who's Your Tailor?" in the script which is now used.

About the same time another artist drew for Mr. Price a picture of a little tailor which soon became a famous trade-mark. The picture of the little tailor was the result of an inspiration gathered from "Samuel Pickwick, Esq., G. C. M. P. C.," in his eulogy on Mr. Tracy Tupman, as portrayed by Charles Dickens in his *Pickwick Papers:*

"Time and feeding had expanded that once romantic form; the black silk waistcoat had become more and more developed; inch by inch had the gold watch chain beneath it disappeared from within the range of Tupman's vision; and gradually had the capacious chin encroached upon the borders of the white cravat."—*Dickens.*

Ed. V. Price & Co., of Chicago, are the proud owners of the "Jolly Little Taylor" and their slogan is still extensively used in their wholesale tailoring business.

CLIQUOT ESKIMO

THE CLIQUOT Club business was established in 1881. The brand is, perhaps, the oldest of all non-alcoholic beverages on the market today in this country. Its trade-mark character, the little "Eskimo Boy," is well entrenched in the minds of the public.

The origin of the "Cliquot Eskimo" dates back to 1911 when the Cliquot Club Company, feeling the need for a trade-mark, began entertaining suggestions for an appropriate trade character for its products. Many ideas were offered—one which received consideration was Punch, of the jovial features; but after considerable deliberation an "Eskimo Boy" was chosen. Mr. I. B. Hazelton, a noted artist of New York City, was selected to paint the "Eskimo Boy" and has continued painting him in various poses for nearly thirty years. The feeling and expression that

113

Mr. Hazelton puts into the "Eskimo Boy's" appearance has been unusual.

The "Cliquot Eskimo" is used in nearly all of the company's advertising and as a trade-mark for its products, which are ginger ale, sparkling water, sarsaparilla, etc.

SEE AMERICA FIRST

THERE'S NEW life in the travel slogan "See America First." War in Europe is blacking out over-seas vacation jaunts. Transportation organizations are bidding for the former European traveler by advertising trips to picturesque places in this country. Soon the question will be asked, "Who first used that slogan, 'See America First'? "

Credit for making the phrase popular belongs to Louis W. Hill, Sr., of St. Paul, who, in 1914, as president of the Great Northern Railway Company, was responsible for splashing the slogan over the entire country in newspaper and billboard advertising. The phrase, accompanied with scenic views and pictures of American Indians, turned a big tide of travel from east to west.

Mr. Hill, son of the Empire Builder, James J. Hill, never has claimed coinage of the slogan. He recalls reading an advertisement in which "see America first" were the last three words of a sentence, and hunting a catch-phrase which would help sell America to Americans, he adopted it as a slogan for his company. Subsequently, the phrase with a picture of a Rocky Mountain Goat, became the Great Northern trade-mark, and for years has been rolling around North America on its freight cars. Mr. Hill tells an anecdote concerning a trip he made in 1914 through Montana's Glacier National Park, acccompanied by a group of newspaper men. The party stopped **on** Gunsight Pass for lunch. Mr. Hill says:

"The view from Gunsight is one of the most magnificent and inspiring in the world. That day, as we sat looking out over the mountains, I thought about the millions of Americans who hadn't seen the grandeurs of their own country. That gave me an idea. One of the guides had a can of paint—why, I don't recall—and I used it to print "See America First" on the face of an immense rock."

THE BELL SYMBOL

THE "BELL" is the symbol for the American Telephone and Telegraph Company and Associated Companies. This well-known trade-mark is the result of an evolution that has extended over a period of almost fifty years. Its origin dates back to the latter part of 1888 when Angus S. Hibbard, after considering a number of other suggested symbols, drew a rough sketch of a bell, across the face of which he printed "Long Distance Telephone."

Mr. Hibbard must have had in mind Alexander Graham Bell, the inventor of the telephone, when he sketched his symbol. If he didn't, it was a happy coincidence.

The "Bell" symbol was at first used solely for the purpose of advertising the location of a long distance telephone. In 1895, the sign was altered to read,

"Local and Long Distance Telephone." At the beginning of the century the blue bell made its appearance, lettered "Local and Long Distance Telephone" and was placed within a double circle in which was printed "American Telephone and Telegraph Co. and Associated Companies." Below the bell appeared the words "Bell System." Many of the Associated Companies adopted the sign for their own use by substituting the names of their companies for the above inscription inside the circle.

The "Bell Symbol" of today, as illustrated, is the same one which was adopted in 1921, with a slight change in lettering and in the appearance of the bell.

In the historical library of the American Telephone and Telegraph Company is the original rough sketch which bears a notation that it was recommended by Mr. Hibbard in December, 1888, and approved by Mr. E. J. Hall, Jr., general manager, on January 8, 1889.

This is an example of a symbolic trade-mark becoming so well known that the owner of the trade-mark (one of the world's largest organizations) is most commonly referred to as the "Bell Telephone Company."

57 VARIETIES

Reg. U. S. Pat. Off.
Reproduced Courtesy of H. J. Heinz Company

MR. H. J. HEINZ, founder of the huge preserved and canned food business operated by H. J. Heinz Company, originated the famous slogan, "57 Varieties."

In the middle nineties, while riding on an elevated train in New York City, Mr. Heinz' attention was attracted to an advertisement of shoes, featuring the expression "21 styles," on an advertising card. It set him thinking, and as he told it: "I said to myself, 'We do not have styles of products, but we do have varieties of products.' Figuring up how many we had I counted 57, and '57' kept coming back into my mind. Seven, seven—there are so many illustrations of the psychological influence of that figure and of its significance to people of all ages and races, that '58 Varieties' or '59 Varieties' did not appeal at all to me as being equally strong. I got off the train immediately, and went down to a lithographer's where I designed a street-car card featuring the phrase '57 Varieties' and had it distributed throughout the United States."

The phrase, "57 Varieties," was adopted in 1896 and registered in 1907. The little green pickle, bearing the name "Heinz," was used as a trade-mark a few years before the phrase, and the Keystone emblem dates back as far as 1878.

Many companies use numerals in connection with their products, but none are better known than the Heinz "57." It has been advertised so well and so long that everybody knows what "57" means.

WALK-OVER

TRADE MARK REG. U.S. PAT. OFF.

Reproduced Courtesy of Geo. E. Keith Company

IT SEEMS strange that a yacht race should have provided the name for a famous shoe, but such is the case.

When Geo. E. Keith began his business career,
in 1874, the so-called specialty shoe was unknown. At
the beginning, a large part of Mr. Keith's output
went to jobbers, who, in turn, sold the shoes to retail-
ers under either the retailer's or the jobber's name.
Mr. Keith realized, however, that this was not the
best method of building up a permanent business as it
left nothing tangible in the way of a following from
the ultimate consumer, so he dropped business rela-
tions with the jobber.

The next step was the adoption of a name for his
product. This presented a great many difficulties.
He did not want to use his own name, as there were
so many Keiths in the shoe business that it would have
been necessary to make a distinction between them,
and this might cause confusion.

It was in the summer of 1898, when the international yacht races were on, that a definite decision was made. Going home from the factory one day, Mr. Keith told his wife of the difficulty he was having in the choice of a name that would be both expressive and appropriate. It chanced that Mrs. Keith was reading the paper, and saw the glaring headline: "American Boat Has a Walk-Over," referring to the yacht race. So she suggested that the shoe be called the "Walk-Over." Mr. Keith at once recognized the possibilities in the name and "Walk-Over" it has been from that day to this.

The Geo. E. Keith Company, of Brockton, Massachusetts, for many years has enjoyed an enviable reputation in the shoe industry, and their "Walk-Over" shoe is an outstanding brand.

1847 ROGERS BROS.

"BORN WITH a silver spoon in her mouth" is a saying used to denote wealth. This expression, prior to 1847, had an actual meaning, because silver spoons were made from solid (coin) silver, and the possession of a few silver spoons was a mark of prosperity. But the phrase began to lose its original meaning in 1847, when three Yankee brothers at Hartford, Connecticut, perfected their electroplating process and began manufacturing silver-plated tableware. Silver-plated spoons, being much less expensive than solid silver, were soon within the reach of more people and were no longer the sign of wealth.

The three Yankee brothers were William, Asa, and Simeon Rogers. They began to work and gain the practical experience of spoon-making in coin silver when quite young, going their divergent ways in the trade; however, in 1847, we find them together in Hartford, Connecticut, under the partnership of Rogers Bros. Applying a process of electroplating in manufacturing silver-plated flatware, their infant business expanded rapidly and their products became well and favorably known. In 1853, the name was changed to Rogers Bros. Mfg. Co.

In 1862, because of financial conditions, their business was sold to Meriden, Connecticut, interests and combined with the Meriden Britannia Company, the largest concern making britannia and silverware at that time in the country. When the business was moved to Meriden, the Rogers brothers joined the Meriden Company organization. In order to make certain that the business in Meriden was known as the direct successor to that started by the Rogers brothers in Hartford in 1847, it was decided by the Meriden Company management and the Rogers brothers to use the date 1847 as part of the trade-mark, and so in November, 1862, the trade-mark became "1847 Rogers Bros.," and thus it remains today. Under the guidance of the financially strong Meriden Company, who, like the Rogers brothers, were firm believers in advertising, the popularity of the "1847 Rogers Bros." brand increased with the years.

About forty years ago, the International Silver Company became the proud owner of this historic trade-mark when it acquired the Meriden Britannia Company along with several other silver companies, and since that time it has continued to aggressively feature "1847 Rogers Bros." in its advertising. The advertising is as colorful today as the attractive pictures of the "1847 Girl," in her quaint old-fashioned costume, which were used early in this century, and which many can recall.

MENNEN FOR MEN

TRADE MARK

Reg. U. S. Pat. Off.
Reproduced Courtesy of The Mennen Company

A MAN'S picture in a circle with the words "TRADE MARK" has appeared on containers of talcum powder for more than half a century. The man in the picture is Mr. Gerhard H. Mennen, founder of The Mennen Company.

Mr. Mennen came to this country from Germany at the age of fifteen. He worked in a drug store a few years after graduating from the New York School of Pharmacy, and then started into business for himself, introducing "Mennen's Talcum Powder," about 1889. He advertised widely and wisely and the growth of his business was the result.

The phrase, "Mennen for Men," has been in use for many years. It originated within the Mennen organization, and was a logical development of a play on words—"Mennen" and "Men" forming a natural tie-up. The Mennen Company has overcome the natural masculine resistance to the use of powder by producing a talcum powder especially for men, emphasizing "Mennen for Men" and subordinating "Talcum." This is sound psychology, and the so-called "he-man" casually purchases a can of "Mennen for Men" without any fear of being thought effeminate.

CARNATION MILK "FROM CONTENTED COWS"

Reg. U. S. Pat. Off.
Reproduced Courtesy of Carnation Company

SEPTEMBER 6, 1939, marked the fortieth birthday of the Carnation Company, which organization was started by Mr. E. A. Stuart, the company's first president and the present chairman of the board. Mr. Stuart did not originate evaporated milk, but he visualized the possibility of economic production and wide distribution of this product. The business began in a primitive condensery in Kent, Washington. Reversing Horace Greeley's advice, "Go west, young man," "Carnation" rapidly expanded eastward and today has large plants and dairy farms scattered throughout the United States and Canada, and their product is nationally and internationally distributed.

But why was the name "Carnation" chosen and the appealing slogan "From Contented Cows" adopted? Here is the founder's own story condensed:

"I wanted an attractive container for the product, a red and white label as a background and a flower as a brand. We had a patent attorney investigate such names as Rose, Poppy, Pansy, Pink, etc., all of which were found to be registered in connection with food products. It was not until after we had an evaporated milk plant operating that I was attracted by a display of cigar boxes bearing the name 'Carnation' in a grocery store in Seattle; I immediately decided this should be our brand name if it could be secured. Fortunately, it was not registered for food products. It was strange that the name had not occurred to me while I was a resident of Los Angeles, where carnations grow out-doors by the acre.

"Before we had any condenseries in the East we found it advisable to employ an advertising agency to help introduce 'Carnation' milk to new markets. On one occasion, Mrs. Helen Shaw Thompson, of New Haven, Connecticut, a copy writer of the advertising agency we had employed, was present when I was describing the ever-verdant pastures where grazed the carefully kept Holstein herds which yielded rich milk for 'Carnation.' I was telling of the picturesque background of these pastures—the snow-capped mountains, from which sparkling streams flowed to the pasture land, and the luxuriant shade trees under which the cows might rest during the heat of the day. Suddenly she exclaimed, 'Oh, the milk of contented cows!' The expression struck all of those present so forcibly that we thereupon decided that would be our slogan—'Carnation Milk From Contented Cows.'"

SLEEP LIKE A KITTEN

Reg. U. S. Pat. Off.
Reproduced Courtesy of Chesapeake and Ohio Lines

A FEW years ago a dyed-in-the-wool railroad official wrote his company, the Chesapeake and Ohio Lines, asking, "Whoever heard of a gol-darned cat advertising a railroad?" The answer now is that millions have heard of it.

The slogan, "Sleep Like a Kitten," was originated by a vice-president of the Chesapeake and Ohio. In June of 1933, a picture entitled "The Sleepy Cat," appeared in a Sunday edition of a New York newspaper. The official ripped it out and held it on his desk for some time while thinking how it might be used in the railroad's advertising. Then he began to ask around the office which best signified sound sleep, "Sleep Like a Top" or "Sleep Like a Kitten." The latter got the majority vote, and the company adopted it as a slogan. An advertisement featuring the cat, having been given the name "Chessie" (apropos of Chesapeake) and carrying the "Sleep Like a Kitten" slogan, appeared in *Fortune Magazine* in the autumn of 1933.

The response to the picture was so spontaneous that exclusive commercial rights were arranged and it was used on the company's 1934 calendar, and each year since a "Chessie" calendar is issued. Framed "Chessie" pictures, cut from these calendars, are to be found in homes far distant from the territory served by the railroad.

Today the company uses "Chessie" and the slogan, "Sleep Like a Kitten," on practically all passenger service advertising, which carries appeal to the fatigued traveler.

BEFORE YOU INVEST—INVESTIGATE

"BEFORE YOU Invest—Investigate" is the slogan for the National Better Business Bureau, Inc., and some fifty-six local Better Business Bureaus located in the principal cities in the United States. This phrase has played an important part in saving the public many millions of dollars. It was suggested by the late Mr. S. P. Halle, president of Halle Brothers, while a member of the board of the Cleveland Better Business Bureau.

In 1920, the executives of the Cleveland Better Business Bureau determined that there was a great need for a plan to protect the uninitiated investor, in addition to the protection afforded by existing legislation. They felt there must be a practical treatment for this economic ailment. In formulating a program they considered these fundamentals—it must be positive, instructive, and preventive. A study was made as to what had been attempted before, and it was found that nearly every old method had worked from a scare-head of DONT'S and BEWARES or from a series of stories that told about crooked schemes, which confused the readers and tended to cast suspicion upon the legitimate business of raising capital.

The plan inaugurated by the Cleveland Better Business Bureau urged the prospective investors, through newspapers and publicity distributed by the banks in Cleveland, to investigate before risking their money. It also furnished investors with a constant flow of information as to the nature of securities that were being offered to the public. The idea was designed to lock the door while the horse was still in the barn, and the appeal was incorporated in the phrase "Before You Invest—Investigate." The slogan was later adopted by all Better Business Bureaus.

HASN'T SCRATCHED YET

Reg. U. S. Pat. Off.
Reproduced Courtesy of The Bon Ami Company

CREDIT FOR the little chick and the phrase, "Hasn't scratched yet," cannot be given to any one individual. It was the result of combined thinking in search of a trade-mark that would attract human interest, and at the same time be closely associated with one of the major selling points of the product. The wisdom of the theory that several minds are better than one was borne out by the selection of this slogan in connection with a cleansing compound.

In 1885, Mr. J. T. Robertson started manufacturing a general line of soaps in Connecticut. He compounded, among other products, a cleaning soap which was designated a mineral soap. Six years later the name of the mineral soap was changed to "Bon Ami" (meaning "good friend" in French) and the soap has proved itself a friend indeed to the housewife. Later the now well-known "Bon Ami" chick, with the words, "Hasn't scratched yet," was adopted as a trade-mark.

The ownership of the "Bon Ami" business changed several times prior to the organization of the present company in 1898.

The results of The Bon Ami Company's operations speak for themselves—today it is estimated that "Bon Ami" can be purchased in nearly every retail food store in the United States, and is sold in more than fifty foreign countries.

In casting its vote for famous trade-marks, the public will not scratch the "Bon Ami" little chick.

PORTLAND CEMENT

WHY IS the word Portland used so often with the word cement? And why do so many manufacturers of the product use Portland in their corporate name?

Portland is not a trade-mark. It is used to define a particular type of cement—a fine, gray product that is used to bond pieces of hard material together to form the stone-like enduring substance which is called concrete.

The name is not derived from Portland, Maine, nor from the largest city in Oregon. It was named after a very famous building stone quarried on the Isle of Portland, properly a peninsula on the coast of Dorchester, England. The first use of the name was made by Joseph Aspdin, a Leeds, England, mason, who, in 1824, produced and patented a particular type of cement and called it Portland, after the well-known rock. His product resembled in color and substance the natural Portland building stone. A half-century before, however, John Smeaton, in constructing the Eddyston Lighthouse, referring to the cement used in the building, said: "It equals the best mercantile Portland stone in solidity and durability." Aspdin's product was used in the construction of the Thames River Tunnel in 1828. His cement, though quite different from the one we have today, was the forerunner of the modern Portland cement.

Until the first Portland cement was made at Coplay, Pennsylvania, in 1872, it was imported from Europe. Not until 1897 did the American volume exceed imports. Today American mills produce and the nation uses more than any other country.

In its more restricted sense, cement, particularly if it is unqualified and used in building and engineering, means Portland cement, and this is by far the most important kind used at the present time, the world's output amounting to millions of tons per annum.

WHITE OWL

Reg. U. S. Pat. Off.
Reproduced Courtesy of General Cigar Co., Inc.

HIGH UP in the list of well-known American cigars roosts the "White Owl." Other familiar brands are—Robt. Burns, Cremo, Roi-tan, Admiration, Webster, Cinco, La Corona, Chancellor, El Producto, Tom Moore, etc.

The "White Owl" was registered as a trade-mark in 1917, but the history of the famous cigar dates back for so many years that there are few living today who can remember its origin. Presidential election bets have been paid off by Owl cigars since soon after the close of the Civil War. The records show that as long ago as 1871 the parent of the General Cigar Co., Inc., produced a cigar known simply as the Owl cigar, and the trade-mark was registered by Straiton and Storm, who are remembered by the elders in the cigar industry. The Owl always has been a favorite brand of cigar.

Today the wings of the "White Owl" cover the universe—the cigar is extensively sold on every continent. It is estimated that during the last two decades approximately five billion "White Owl" cigars have been smoked. The advertising of the General Cigar Co., Inc., in recent years has added materially to its popularity and consumption.

TANGLEFOOT

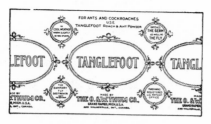

Reg. U. S. Pat. Off.
Reproduced Courtesy of The Tanglefoot Company

THE TWO Thum brothers, Otto and William, were clerking in their father's drug store at Grand Rapids, Michigan, in the summer of 1886. The ways and means for a college education was their problem.

It was a custom in those day for druggists to make fly paper for their retail trade, a few sheets at a time. It was a messy task, and the Thum drug store preferred to purchase its requirements from a competitor. Otto is credited with suggesting to his brother that they make fly paper for all the drug stores in the city, and without parental approval or encouragement the boys launched their business venture in the rear of their father's store.

William, a student of chemistry, was not satisfied with the old formula. It dried too quickly and soaked through the paper. He experimented in search of a better formula. Finally, he discovered that by glue sizing the paper before applying the sticky compound the soaking problem could be solved; he also found that two sheets could be placed with their sticky surfaces together. Other improvements were made and the formula was patented in 1887. These discoveries paved the way for the fly paper's phenomenal growth.

It is believed that the product was called "Tanglefoot" almost from the beginning as the records disclose this trade-mark was registered the same year the formula was patented. The name was obviously chosen because of the sticky material tangling the feet of the flies when it caught them.

In the early days, the business was operated as a partnership of the Thum brothers, but later was incorporated as O. & W. Thum Co. This name was continued until 1924. At that time "Tanglefoot" had become so well known, and as most persons referred to the business as the "Tanglefoot Company," it was deemed advisable to rename the business "The Tanglefoot Company."

"Tanglefoot" fly paper is only one of the company's many products. It is now engaged in a general insecticide business; but if you visited its laboratory and witnessed the actual raising of more than 25,000 flies every year for experimental purposes, you could not help but associate "Tanglefoot" with flies.

QUAKER OATS

Reg. U. S. Pat. Off.
Reproduced Courtesy of The Quaker Oats Company

THE LITTLE "Quaker" in the costume in vogue during the time of William Penn, with his package of "Quaker Oats" in one hand and his scroll of purity in the other, has long endeared himself to the public.

The "Quaker" mark was originally registered in the name of the American Cereal Company in 1895, and assigned to The Quaker Oats Company in 1906.

An official, searching the dictionary for an appropriate name, found nothing which especially appealed to him and turned to the Encyclopedia and became interested in reading an article on the Quakers. The purity of the lives of the people, their sterling honesty, their strength and manliness impressed him. The parallel between their characteristics and what was needed in character and principle in a new business, if it were to be successful, caught his imagination. He reached the conclusion that "Quaker" was the name to use, and his associates agreed with him.

The Quaker Oats Company has consistently used the little "Quaker" in their advertising as an emblem of the purity and wholesomeness which is so characteristic of their product.

FRIGIDAIRE

FOR THOUSANDS of years civilized man had no refrigeration save the little he was able to obtain from
ice and snow. Mechanical refrigeration did not
make its appearance until the nineteenth century, and
for more than fifty years was confined to the manufacture of ice in central plants. Electrical refrigeration and air conditioning, which are such important
factors in our lives today, are achievements of this
century, and "Frigidaire" is the best known name in
the industry.

The "Frigidaire" line of household and commercial equipment had its beginning in 1916 with the incorporation of the Guardian Frigerator Company
in Detroit. Fifty machines were built and sold during
the first year. During the war the new business found
it difficult to raise additional capital. As a result it
was sold, in 1918, to William C. Durant, who took it
over as a personal investment. A few months later the
company was changed to The Frigidaire Corporation, taking the new name which had been given the
product. "Frigidaire" was chosen as the name because it seemed the ideal word to describe the product
—it tells the story adequately, is easy to remember and
lends itself nicely to advertising.

Mr. Durant, after owning the business for about a
year, sold it to General Motors. Its operations expanded rapidly and electrical refrigeration was

applied to various uses. One of its most important ventures was in 1931, when it entered the field of air conditioning. Today the company is the world's largest builder of refrigerating and air conditioning equipment.

Reproduced Courtesy of Simmons Company

BACK IN the dark ages man slept in trees to protect himself from beasts of prey. Beds used centuries ago were ornate but far from comfortable. Solomon's bed was made of cedar of Lebanon; Cleopatra's was of ivory and gold. It was not until about the time of our Civil War, however, that bed springs came to be used. At the beginning of the twentieth century, inventors began experimenting with the inter-spring mattress. In 1925, the Simmons Company placed on the market a new kind of mattress and called it "Beautyrest." It is estimated that today over 3,000,000 people sleep on "Beautyrests."

The officials of the Simmons Company, after a careful survey of many submitted names, chose "Beautyrest" for the reason they believed that name was most applicable to a high-grade mattress, which afforded the most comfort for restful sleep. The name was registered as a trade-mark in January, 1926.

The Simmons Company is in its sixty-ninth manufacturing year. Its famous "Owl" trade-mark with the slogan, "1/3 of your Life is Spent in Bed," has been continually used since 1901. But "Beautyrest" is now the company's best known trade-mark and the mattress is the outstanding Simmons product. In fact, it is the largest selling mattress in the world.

SUNKIST

THE CALIFORNIA Fruit Growers Exchange is a coöperative marketing organization and has been in existence for nearly fifty years. It has stood the test of time and is owned today by three-fourths of all the citrus growers in California and Arizona.

"Sunkist" is the emblem of the Exchange and the name is used in its advertising to create an increasing consumer demand for the products of its members.

Desultory efforts at local advertising were made practically from the inception of the Exchange, but it was not until 1907 that systematic advertising began. In that year, the management authorized an expenditure of $10,000 for the advertising of citrus fruits. At that time, the Exchange had a president who was a firm believer in advertising, Mr. F. Q. Storey.

Mr. Storey consulted with his friend, Mr. E. O. McCormick, of the Southern Pacific, whose faith in the soundness of advertising was such that he told Mr. Storey that for every dollar the Exchange expended in advertising, the railway he represented would spend an equal amount. Armed with this generous offer the Exchange proceeded to spend the $10,000.

Iowa was selected as the experimenting ground. Fruit went forward in special bannered trains. Prizes were offered for articles that could be used in advertising California oranges and lemons. The slogan, "Oranges for Health—California for Wealth," was bill-boarded throughout the state by the railroad. At the same time the Exchange, in an endeavor to identify and popularize its products, shipped the fruit in distinctive boxes imprinted with "California Fruit Growers Exchange" and widely advertised the name and package. That this was potent advertising is evidenced by the way the Iowans not only bought the fruit but also migrated to California in search of the advertised health and wealth.

In July, 1907, Mr. R. C. Brandon, of the Exchange Advertising Agency, recommended that a trademark be advertised instead of the name of the organization, and he suggested, "S-U-N-K-I-S-S-E-D," which he soon changed to "S-U-N-K-I-S-T." The following spring the board of directors of the Exchange adopted as a trade-mark for the best grades of fruit the word, "Sunkist."

The organization maintains a field staff of inspectors, who visit the packing houses and coöperate with the management of the houses in seeing that only fruit complying with certain standards goes to the market labeled "Sunkist."

The California Fruit Growers Exchange today is one of our largest advertisers and "Sunkist" appears not only in newspapers, magazines, etc., but on the fruit itself.

GOING! GOING!! GONE!!!

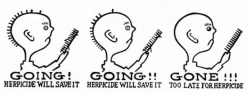

Reg. U. S. Pat. Off.
Reproduced Courtesy of The Herpicide Co.

THE UNIQUE trade-mark, "Going! Going!! Gone!!!," has been associated with Herpicide for over forty years.

At the time it made its first appearance there was very little censorship on false and misleading advertising. Many manufacturers of hair and scalp preparations were exploiting their products to the gullible public by extravagant statements. As an illustration, one company used a picture of a woman with long hair with the accompanying caption, "grew this hair and we can prove it."

Dr. Newbro coined the trade-mark, "Going! Going!! Gone!!!," for his dandruff germ remedy known as "Newbro's Herpicide." The doctor believed that in order to combat the unfair practices of his competitors, the keynote for his advertising should be "truth in advertising." He laid emphasis on the fact that his product would save hair rather than grow hair, and he let the slogan, "Going! Going!! Gone!!!," tell the story of hair and scalp neglect.

Since the adoption of the Herpicide trade-mark it has been the basis of all The Herpicide Co.'s advertising claims. Most of the unscrupulous advertisers have fallen by the wayside, but Dr. Newbro's product has been a leader in the field for more than four decades.

WATCH THE FORDS GO BY

WHEN YOU see the slogan, "Watch the Fords Go By," naturally you think it is an advertisement for automobiles. It was originally a baseball cry. Years ago the old Highland Park factory of the Ford Motor Company had a ball team. The field quarters of the team was a round bell tent, with its low walls rolled up for ventilation. During a Saturday afternoon game a shower came on. The officials took shelter in the tent, but the game went on regardless of the shower. The Ford team was at bat and they must have been hitting that day for there was a steady stream of Ford runners to first. The men in the tent could see the red striped stockings of the Ford runners twinkling past in the rain. And one man exclaimed: "Watch the Fords go by! Just watch the Fords go by!" Someone picked it up and applied it to the car as a slogan.

This effective phrase, "Watch the Fords Go By," was first used by the Ford Motor Company in 1908, at the time of the introduction of the Model "T" car, and millions of Fords have gone by since that time.

Mr. Henry Ford completed his first automobile in 1896, and the present company was organized in 1903. The phenomenal growth of the business and the story of Mr. Ford, one of America's great industrial leaders, is known to all.

WHITE ROCK

YEARS BEFORE white men realized the value of the mineral springs at Waukesha, Wisconsin, Indians had camped there and enjoyed the waters. In 1871, the owner of the property, Mr. H. M. Colver, gave the spring the name "White Rock" because of the natural magnesian rock basin from which the spring flowed. During the seventies and eighties, Waukesha was developed into a resort and known as the "Saratoga of the West." Towards the close of the century, "White Rock" began to be used as a table water and its popularity rapidly spread. By 1900, "White Rock" was being exported to Europe and other continents, and it was served at the Coronation banquet of Edward VII in 1901. The next year an English press notice told that King Edward used it to dilute his wines.

During the World's Fair in Chicago, in 1893, the

painting of the Greek Goddess, Psyche, at Nature's Mirror (the work of Paul Thurman, an outstanding artist of that day) was exhibited. Impressed with the beauty of this painting, typifying sparkling youth and purity, the White Rock Company acquired the rights to the picture as a trade-mark and it has appeared on all "White Rock" labels ever since.

The White Rock Mineral Springs Company, which has owned and operated the mineral springs since 1913, has become favorably known for its unique advertising. Its phrase, "on the alkaline side," received public acceptance instantly.

"White Rock" is now synonymous with sparkling water the world over and Waukesha itself has gained international recognition, since each bottle of water carries the words, "Bottled only at the springs, Waukesha, Wis."

AN APPLE A DAY

"SCIENTISTS FIND that your 'Apple-a-day' does most good when you eat it fresh." The foregoing is an extract from an advertisement appearing in the December, 1939, issue of *Good Housekeeping Magazine*. The advertisement was sponsored by the Washington State Apple Commission. Apple growers in this country for years have been advertising the health value of apples, often twitting the doctor in various rhymes, such as "An apple a day keeps the doctor away." In recent years, however, apple associations have advertised the advisability of an apple daily in the diet, and its importance in regard to health without tantalizing the medical profession by the doctor-apple rhymes.

The rhyme, "An apple a day keeps the doctor away," with its ancient implication of therapy, goes back scores and probably hundreds of years in different countries where apples were used for various cures. The old Devonshire form:

> Ate an apfel avore gwain to bed
> Makes the Doctor beg his bread

echoes an ancient custom of saluting apple trees on Christmas Eve. In some sections of England this ceremony is still performed. Processions visit the principal orchards of a parish, select one tree in each orchard, salute it and sprinkle it with cider to insure a plentiful crop.

The phrase, "An Apple a Day," which had its origin from the rhymes about the doctor and the apple, has played a major role in making the public apple-health conscious in this country.

BODY BY FISHER

Reg. U. S. Pat. Off.
Reproduced Courtesy of General Motors Corporation,
Fisher Body Div.

THE FISHER Body emblem was used in national advertising for the first time in 1922. It was chosen because it represented the finest in coach craft in pre-automobile times. It is the composite of two Napoleonic coaches—one used at the marriage of Princess Marie Louise, of Austria, to Napoleon, and the other being the coronation coach of Napoleon.

Sons of a blacksmith and carriage maker, Fred and Charles Fisher, started a business of making automobile bodies under the name of the Fisher Body Company, at Detroit, Michigan, in 1908. The closed car at that time was little more than an experiment. A rich man's hobby, built by hand at excessive cost, its use was limited principally to the wealthy for city driving. Their first large order was from Cadillac, in 1910, for one hundred and fifty closed bodies, and from that time on their business expanded rapidly. Credit for the development of the closed body, as we know it today, belongs to the Fisher brothers and few people realize that they also produced the first four-door body.

In 1919, General Motors purchased 60 per cent interest in the Fisher Body Corporation. At the same time, arrangements were made by Fisher to supply all of General Motors' passenger car body requirements. Shortly after this, Fisher acquired the Fleetwood Body Corporation. In 1926, General Motors purchased the outstanding interest in Fisher Body which then became a division of the corporation. It is now the largest manufacturer of automobile bodies in the world.

KOTEX
KLEENEX

KOTEX Sanitary Napkins

"GIVE US more absorbent" was the plea from surgeons and nurses in the field hospitals of France during the World War, when each recurring wave of battle brought in more wounded. Cellucotton absorbent wadding was an answer to this plea and it was ordered from America in such quantities that the mills were built "rush" to produce it in shipload lots. War nurses saw the possibilities of this absorbent product, and after the Armistice their suggestions were utilized in the production of a wonderful convenience for women, known as "Kotex." The name was coined and meant nothing, yet after its appearance on the market a woman could ask for "Kotex" without embarrassment and get exactly what she wanted.

KLEENEX Disposable Tissues

After "Kotex" had been on the market about three years, the manufacturer learned that people were using the cellulose layers of "Kotex" pads for removing cold cream and cosmetics. So a new field was opened, and the product, "Kleenex," appeared in 1924. It was quickly accepted by the public and soon used for different purposes, such as colds, hay-fever, etc. The name "Kleenex" was also coined, and simulated "Kotex" in order to keep it in the family.

The International Cellucotton Products Co., manufacturer of these products and owner of these trademarks, has performed an outstanding feat in advertising and merchandising "Kotex" and "Kleenex."

BUSTER BROWN

Reg. U. S. Pat. Off.
Reproduced Courtesy of Brown Shoe Company

AT THE beginning of the twentieth century, the newspaper comics were just beginning to be popular. Among the pioneers was Mr. R. F. Outcault, an artist connected with the *New York Herald,* who created the character of Buster Brown and his dog, Tige. Buster was a mischievous, fun-loving youngster with the happy faculty of getting into all sorts of trouble and then landing on both feet when things seemed the darkest. Each cartoon strip would end up with Buster either pointing to or writing a resolution as to his adventures or misdeeds of the day.

In 1904, the Brown Shoe Company purchased from the artist the right to use "Buster Brown" for shoes. It was a natural tie-up for children's shoes and the company capitalized on the popularity of Buster and Tige by effective advertising. Buster Brown is so well known that the Brown Shoe Company is often referred to as the "Buster Brown Shoe Company."

It is one of the oldest names of children's shoes in

the country. In fact, there were very few names associated with shoes when the Brown Shoe Company started using "Buster Brown."

In recent years, Buster's clothing has been somewhat modernized. The company has discontinued using the whole body and now only shows the head and shoulders of both boy and dog.

Buster and Tige, idolized by young and old, certainly have earned their place in the trade-mark Hall of Fame.

ETHYL GASOLINE

"ETHYL" APPEARS on more gasoline filling station pumps in this country than any other trade-mark. The name is derived from tetraethyl lead and not from the feminine name, Ethel.

The "Ethyl Gasoline" trade-mark was designed under the supervision of the scientists who had discovered the effectiveness of tetraethyl lead as an anti-knock in gasoline, Thomas Midgley, Jr., and C. F. Kettering, both of whom at the time were employees of the General Motors Corporation. The General Motors Chemical Company were the first marketers of "Ethyl" Fluid and licensors to other companies for the manufacture and sale of "Ethyl Gasoline."

Application for the "Ethyl Gasoline" trade-mark was filed in 1923. A year later the trade-mark was registered and assigned to the General Motors Chemical Company. Shortly after the incorporation of the Ethyl Gasoline Corporation, in 1924, they purchased the assets of the General Motors Chemical Company, and the "Ethyl Gasoline" trade-mark was assigned to the Ethyl Corporation.

When the motorist asks at the filling station for highest anti-knock or "high-test" gasoline, the attendant knows that he means "Ethyl."

OLD DUTCH CLEANSER

Reg. U. S. Pat. Off.
Reproduced Courtesy of The Cudahy Packing Company

IN MARCH, 1905, The Cudahy Packing Company placed on the market a cleaning product introduced by the trade-mark of an Old Dutch girl, and the slogan, "Chases Dirt." The inspiration for the trademark came from a picture of a little Dutch scene with a Holland Goose girl embossed in the corner of the frame. As Holland is known the country over for its cleanliness, it was thought the Dutch girl would be an appropriate feature of a trade-mark for a cleaning product. It had all the essentials of human interest, strength, simplicity, and, in addition, was very striking and had a certain romantic appeal. The figure of the Holland girl was altered into that of a Dutch matron. The name, "Old Dutch Cleanser," and the slogan, "Chases Dirt," naturally followed.

Today, the aggressive poise of the Old Dutch girl, with the upraised stick, depicting the severe and uncompromising attitude toward dirt, is not only nationally known throughout the United States, but is universally known throughout the entire world.

THE PRUDENTIAL HAS THE STRENGTH
OF GIBRALTAR

Reg. U. S. Pat. Off.
*Reproduced Courtesy of The Prudential Insurance
Company of America*

THE ROCK of Gibraltar is first mentioned in literature about 500 B.C. by Pindar, the Greek poet, as one of the pillars of Hercules, the other pillar being opposite on the coast of Africa. Ptolemy, the Egyptian geographer, and Pliny, the Elder, also referred to it. There is no record and no evidence of any settlement on the Rock until the eighth century of the Christian era. Since that time it has been the object of conquest by many warring tribes and nations. Early in the eighteenth century the British seized the Rock from Spain and ever since it has remained a British possession. The impregnability of Gibraltar seems to have been established during the great siege of 1779-1783 which withstood all attacks by Spain in their endeavor to recapture the Rock. At the present time the entire Rock is under a military form of govern-

167

ment, and the importance of Gibraltar may be gauged by the fact that practically every nation has a diplomatic representative there.

When The Prudential Insurance Company of America adopted as a slogan the phrase, "The Prudential has the Strength of Gibraltar," sagacious advertising men declared that it would become one of the most valuable advertising phrases ever coined. Gibraltar's strength was known to almost every man, woman, and child in the civilized world. To associate this known strength with a great financial institution was a happy stroke of advertising skill. The contour of the trade-mark was taken from a photograph of the Rock of Gibraltar itself and never has been changed since the date of its original adoption in 1896.

The picture and slogan have been extensively used by The Prudential Company in its advertising, and the trade-mark appears on every insurance policy issued. It is perhaps one of the most effective trademarks ever conceived, as the picture tells the story better than words.

KNOX GELATINE

Reg. U. S. Pat. Off.
Reproduced Courtesy of Charles B. Knox
Gelatine Co., Inc.

THE MAN who built the first steam locomotive in America was the originator of gelatin—Peter Cooper, famous inventor and philanthropist. As long ago as 1845 he filed specifications with the United States Patent Office for the making of "a transparent, concentrated substance containing all the ingredients fitting it for table use and requiring only the addition of hot water to dissolve it so that it may be poured into moulds and when cold will be fit for use." Mr. Cooper took no steps to merchandise his gelatin before he died, in 1883.

A few years later, "Knox Gelatine" was placed on the market and soon the little calf's head emblem appeared as its trade-mark. The founder of "Knox Gelatine," Charles B. Knox, selected the calf's head for a trade-mark because the product at the beginning was made from calf stock instead of bone stock as at present. Mr. Knox was the first gelatin manufacturer to produce it in granulated form.

In recent years, Charles B. Knox Gelatine Co., Inc., owner of the calf's head trade-mark, has added pictures of black and white chefs, carrying platters of molded sparkling gelatin. This new trade-mark is used extensively, but the calf's head is shown alone on the outside of the packaged product.

To the American housewife, opening her kitchen cupboard, the little calf's head appears as a familiar friend.

THOMAS A. EDISON SIGNATURE

Reg. U. S. Pat. Off.
*Reproduced Courtesy of Thomas A. Edison,
Incorporated*

THE WORLD'S most famous signature trade-mark is the name in autographic script of America's greatest inventor, the late Thomas A. Edison.

Thomas A. Edison, Incorporated, is the owner of numerous registrations of the "Thomas A. Edison signature" trade-mark for goods in various classes. Records disclose that the first use of the signature trade-mark was in 1897. One of the earliest registrations was dated June 19, 1900, and granted to Thomas A. Edison personally. It was later assigned to Thomas A. Edison, Incorporated, and renewed by the company in 1930. The class of merchandise covered by the registration was scientific and philosophical apparatus.

The "Thomas A. Edison signature" trade-mark is still extensively used by Thomas A. Edison, Incorporated, and its various associated companies. This trade-mark not only identifies the particular product to which it is attached, but reminds the public of the great achievements of the immortal inventor. Among the products so identified are the following: Dictating machines; photographic record blanks; storage batteries; primary batteries, including dry cells; miners' electric lighting outfits, and other portable

171

electric lighting outfits; electronic and audio apparatus and devices, including audio amplifiers, microphones, oscillators and attenuators; fire detectors; electrical switches; and electrical relays.

LISTERINE

THE TRADE name "Listerine" was registered in June, 1881, by the Lambert Pharmacal Company. It was named after Lord Lister, who was familiar with the product "Listerine" Antiseptic.

Lord Lister was a famous English surgeon and founder of antiseptic surgery. In his first experiment, in 1865, upon a compound fracture, Lister used undiluted carbolic acid. The experiment was a success but the caustic properties of carbolic acid injured tissues and made it unsuitable for general surgery. After experimenting for several years, he blended the carbolic acid with inert substances and obtained a most satisfactory result.

"Listerine," like Lord Lister's developed product, is an antiseptic which is not harmful to tissues, and it was fitting to honor Lord Lister by naming this product after him.

The Lambert Pharmacal Company, in addition to their manufacturing laboratories in this country, maintain manufacturing laboratories in Canada, England, Australia, New Zealand, France, Spain, Holland, Switzerland, Cuba, Mexico, Chile, Argentina, and China, and their products are sold throughout the world.

20 MULE TEAM

ONE OF the most novel and interesting attractions at the St. Louis Exposition, in 1904, was the 20 Mule Borax Team, which the Pacific Coast Borax Company brought from Death Valley, that famous region of desolation where so many human beings have perished. It was difficult for spectators to appreciate the fact that this was the same type of mule team and the identical huge wagon which regularly transported borax from Death Valley to the railroad, some one hundred and sixty miles distant, over a trail leading across barren wastes and scorching sand, the temperature ranging from 130° to 150° during part of the trip. "20 Mule Team" caravans transported borax for many years before giving way to the iron horse and modern railroad, but in the meantime, the romantic picture of "20 Mule Team" became one of the most famous trade-marks in the history of America.

The "20 Mule Team" trade-mark was originally applied for in 1894 by a predecessor-in-interest of the Pacific Coast Borax Company, but the trade-mark application discloses that the "20 Mule Team" brand had been known and used since 1891. The original application only covered borax, but, in 1896, the trade-mark was extended to cover boric acid, soap products, boron compounds, etc.

Commercially, borax is today extensively used in various industries, such as the manufacture of enamel, pottery, glass, textiles, leather, and paper. Different compounds and derivatives of borax are also packaged in popular sizes for household uses, under the familiar brand name and trade-mark, "20 Mule Team." The varied uses of these borax products have become widely known and practically indispensable in the modern household.

HOLEPROOF

THE HOLEPROOF Hosiery Co. manfactures men's and women's hosiery of all kinds, which are sold widely in this country and abroad.

In a decision rendered many years ago, the Circuit Court of Appeals for the Second Circuit, referring to the name "Holeproof" said: "It has acquired a secondary meaning, indicating to the prospective purchaser, not that socks sold under it are indestructible, but that they are those which complainant has been making and supplying to customers, apparently to their entire satisfaction." The name was chosen by the founder forty-two years ago. The origin of the business dates back to 1872, in Kalamazoo, Michigan, when Mr. Carl Freschl, under the name of the Kalamazoo Knitting Works, started making stockings with a crude hand knitting machine.

In 1882, Mr. Freschl moved his factory to Milwaukee. Towards the close of the nineteenth century, after experimenting with a new spinning yarn developed in England, he was successful in manufacturing a product superior to others on the market. Up to this time, stockings and socks had been made with the emphasis on appearance and without much regard to durability. A trade-mark which would feature the wearing qualities of the new product was desired and after considering many names Mr. Feschl chose "Holeproof" because it suggested to the purchaser the idea of durability and dependability.

In 1904, the Holeproof Hosiery Co. was incorporated and took over the business of the Kalamazoo Company, and, in 1906, "Holeproof" was registered as a trade-mark.

There has always been a question as to who owns the hole in the doughnut, but there is no question as to who owns the right to use the word "Holeproof" in the hosiery industry. The Holeproof Hosiery Co. has successfully prevented the use and registration by others of such names as No-Hole, Sta-Hole, Hole-Less, Hole-Shy, and No-Mo-Hole.

CAMPBELL KIDS

Eat your Campbell's daily—
Then you'll be
Healthy, strong and happy—
Just like me!

Reg. U. S. Pat. Off.
Reproduced Courtesy of Campbell Soup Company

THE CAMPBELL Soup Company had its inception in 1869, when Joseph Campbell and Abram A. Anderson, under the firm name of Anderson and Campbell, established a canning and preserving plant at Camden, New Jersey. The building is still standing and in active use by the Campbell Soup Company today. In 1891, the business started by Messrs. Campbell and Anderson was incorporated under the name of The Joseph Campbell Preserve Company, which was later changed to the Campbell Soup Company.

From the beginning, their canned products achieved a favorable reputation, but it was the introduction, in 1897, of canned soup which gave the great impetus to the business. Credit for the canned soup must be given to Dr. John T. Dorrance, who, for many years, was the financial and merchandising genius of the company. The germ of the idea of selling canned soup was planted in Dr. Dorrance's mind when he was a chemistry student in a German university, and observed the importance of soup in the diet of the people in Continental Europe.

Advertising has been a large factor in the growth of the Campbell Soup Company, in which the "Campbell Kids" have played a prominent part. Their origin dates back to the beginning of the century, when the company was embarking on a program of street car card advertising. A figure was desired which would typify robust health, to which wholesome foods contribute so materially; and with the coöperation of the Ketterlinus Lithographic Manufacturing Company, of Philadelphia, the "Campbell Kids" were born. For nearly forty years these colorful little figures, with their antics and gay verses, have brightened advertising.

THE WATCH THAT MADE THE
DOLLAR FAMOUS

THE INGERSOLL watch first appeared in 1892, and soon thereafter the unique slogan, "The Watch That Made the Dollar Famous," caught the imagination of the American people.

This is the story of its origin: It appears that Mr. R. H. Ingersoll was at a social function, and in the receiving line the hostess was about to introduce him to the guest of honor; she had a lapse of memory and introduced him by another name. In catching herself she became flustered, still could not think of the name, and finally blurted out, "Oh, the man that made the dollar famous." Mr. Ingersoll was quick to see that he was better known in connection with the dollar watch than by his name, so the next day he presented his company with the slogan, "The Watch That Made the Dollar Famous."

The dollar may be deflated or inflated, but the undeviating value of the slogan, "The Watch That Made the Dollar Famous," now owned by The Ingersoll-Waterbury Co., will remain.

THE 606TH experiment clicked— and the product that emerged became universally known as "606." Its other name is "Salvarsan" (soul saver). The chemical designation is something like "Diamino-dihydroxyarsenobenzene-dihydrochloride."

In 1907, Paul Ehrlich, famous German bacteriologist, discovered the dye known as "trypan red," which, when injected into the blood of animals infected with trypanosomes (sleeping sickness) effected the destruction of these organisms. This led him to try to treat other diseases by chemical injections, and culminated with his famous discovery for treating venereal diseases. It was announced in 1910 that he had prepared an arsenical compound, known as "606" or "Salvarsan," which was a treatment for syphilis.

The product was instantly a huge commercial success. From the inventor's laboratory in Germany, over 65,000 doses of the product went out to all parts of the world during the first year it was on the market. Sales soon mounted into the hundreds of thousands. Ehrlich and his associates never missed an opportunity for publicity, and their advertising statements, judged by today's standards of the medical profession, might be considered unethical.

In this country, "606" was registered as a trademark in September, 1911, although the product was more frequently sold here under the name "Salvarsan." Until the first World War, Germany was the sole source of supply. Then came the blockade, and because of the scarcity of "Salvarsan" its price soared in the United States until it reached $100 for a single dose. As the war continued, American chemists developed a similar formula which they called "Arsphenamine." In the past twenty years, several other compounds used in treating syphilis and based on the "Salvarsan" principle have emerged from American laboratories. These refined products are sold under various names and for less than $1 a dose, but "606" has been so well established in the public mind that it has become a synonym for cures of syphilis.

IRON FIREMAN

Reproduced Courtesy of Iron Fireman Manufacturing Company

FROM A few bolts, nuts, and scraps of iron emerged a famous name and trade-mark—"Iron Fireman."

In 1923, Mr. C. T. Burg, sales manager of the Portland Wire and Iron Works, took a rough sketch of an automatic coal stoker, in the form of a crudely constructed robot, to the company's advertising agency and asked Mr. Joseph Gerber's assistance in preparing a circular on a new product which he called a stoker. Mr. Gerber never had heard of the contraption and during the interview referred to it as an "iron fireman." This name immediately caught Mr. Burg's fancy and it soon became the company's trade-mark and later was incorporated into the company's name.

Today the public is well acquainted with the name "Iron Fireman," as well as the robot shoveling coal and spouting steam from its nostrils, symbolic of the automatic coal stoker made by the Iron Fireman Manufacturing Company, of Portland, Oregon.

"Iron Fireman" is one of the most successful recent trade-marks, largely due to its effective suggestiveness —the name and robot supplanting human labor.

THE HAM WHAT AM

IN SO FAR AS the records and memories of Armour and Company's executives reveal, their slogan, "The Ham What Am," accompanied by a picture of a negro chef, was suggested by a lithographer on a display sketch, submitted some forty or fifty years ago. This typical negro expression, coupled with the fact that a colored man is notably a good judge of ham, instantly caught the fancy of the company's officials. From the time of the slogan's inception it has been used continuously in the company's advertising, except for a short period in the twenties, when it was thought that the phrase was outmoded. It was revived in 1930 and has been used since that time.

Perhaps no trade-mark nor slogan has been the base of more stories and jokes, with the possible exception of the famous Smith Brothers, Trade and Mark. One of the most often told stories is that of a newspaper, during a political campaign, running a picture of a candidate whom they were opposing, beside an advertisement of Armour and Company featuring the slogan, "The Ham What Am." These stories and jokes are good advertising value to an established leader in its field. It is said that Ford welcomed the stories on his Model-T.

Armour and Company, world famous meat packers, recently promoted the negro chef, who made his debut with "The Ham What Am," to the status of a trade-mark figure for all of Armour's meat products.

REXALL

THIRTY-NINE YEARS ago, forty retail druggists embarked upon a coöperative business venture, and
called their stores "Rexall." The originator of the
plan was a traveling salesman from Detroit, Louis
K. Liggett, founder and president of the United
Drug Company. The idea was a huge success. There
are now in existence more than eleven thousand
"Rexall" drug stores, and not a single one of the
original forty druggists has relinquished his "Rexall"
agency.

The trade-mark, "Rexall," is protected by over
thirty United States trade-mark registrations and is
registered in many foreign countries. Its origin is as
follows:

After organizing the United Drug Company, in
1902, Mr. Liggett wanted a name for his first line of
remedies. Through a mutual friend he was introduced to Walter Jones Willson, a young Boston man
"who liked to handle words." Mr. Liggett explained
that the name must be short, distinctive, original,
easily pronounced and remembered, look well in
type, be registerable as a trade-mark, and have a definite meaning. Mr. Willson, now editor of the
United Drug Company's monthly institutional magazine, submitted to Mr. Liggett a list of about fifty
coined words, including the name "Rexall," which he
made by combining the Latin word "Rex" and the

English word "all," this name being accompanied with the explanatory slogan, "King of All." The name, "Rexall," was adopted, and in the early days the slogan was coupled with it in the company's advertisements until the public had learned the significance of the name.

"Rexall" is the principal trade-mark for the United Drug Company's various products, and, since its inception, has been used extensively in the company's merchandising efforts. The United Drug Company is perhaps the largest manufacturer of drug items in the world, over five thousand different articles being listed in its line.

LOG CABIN SYRUP

Reg. U. S. Pat. Off.
Reproduced Courtesy of General Foods Corporation

BECAUSE OF his frontier fame and the story that he served hard cider instead of wine in his home, a part of which had been a log cabin, the political cry for William Harrison, the Whig candidate for President in 1840, was "Log cabin and hard cider." During Harrison's popularity many traders sold their products in containers shaped to form miniature log cabins. The one that, perhaps, attracted the most attention was E. G. Booz's Old Cabin Whiskey, sold in a glass bottle in the form of a log cabin. It is believed that the name "booze" for whiskey originated from Mr. Booz's product. But during the last half century the most familiar product sold under the name, "Log Cabin," and in a container in the shape of a log cabin, is syrup.

In 1887, a Minnesota wholesale grocer, Mr. P. J. Towle, conceived the idea of selling syrup in a container instead of the unsanitary bulk method from a barrel. He was an ardent admirer of Abraham Lincoln, log cabin born, so he named the syrup which he had blended from cane and maple sugar "Log Cabin," and designed a tin container in the shape of a log cabin. His business was merged with General Foods in 1927.

For many years the little "Log Cabin" container has been known nearly everywhere, the syrup being a favorite brand. Its popularity has been materially increased by the extensive advertising given it by General Foods in the past ten years.

THE SKIN YOU LOVE TO TOUCH

FROM ADVERTISING written thirty years ago for Woodbury's Facial Soap, six words took life as the slogan, "The Skin You Love to Touch."

In 1910, the sale of Woodbury's Facial Soap had shrunk badly. Competitive brands sold largely on the basis of their medicinal properties. The largest seller of toilet soap was a low priced soap that sold mainly as a cleanser. Women were interested, not so much in soap as such, but in what it would do for their skins. The manufacturers of Woodbury's Facial Soap believed their product warranted its promotion on the basis that it did something more than cleanse, and their advertising agency provided the phrase that caught the public fancy, "The Skin You Love to Touch."

This slogan first appeared as part of a sentence in Woodbury's advertising, prepared by the Cincinnati office of the J. Walter Thompson Company. In describing the expected benefits from the use of Woodbury's Facial Soap, such expressions as "a soft skin," "a smooth skin," "a beautiful skin," seemed threadbare. Hackneyed expressions wouldn't do. But the phrase, "The Skin You Love to Touch," told the story—particularly when used with drawings of beautiful women by popular artists of the day, such as Henry Hutt.

Woodbury's Facial Soap has been on the market

for more than sixty years. It was first produced by Dr. John H. Woodbury, whose "beauty parlor" was established in 1870 at Albany, New York. It was purchased by the Andrew Jergens Company in 1901.

In the years that followed the introduction of the famous slogan, "The Skin You Love to Touch," Andrew Jergens Company's business has rapidly expanded, and Woodbury's Facial Soap increased in popularity.

BAKELITE

BAKELITE

Reg. U. S. Pat. Off.
Reproduced Courtesy of Bakelite Corporation

OXYBENZYLMETHYLENGLYCOLANHYDRIDE was the chemical name for the first thermosetting plastic material discovered by Dr. Leo Hendrik Baekeland, in 1907. The product is the combination of two common chemicals—phenol and formaldehyde. The chemical name, however, was too much of a mouthful for even technical men, so Dr. Baekeland decided to name his discovery after himself, "Bakelite."

The origin of the Bakelite Trefoil trade-mark is not one of glamour, but a planned design to evolve a symbol which would incorporate all the elements of a good trade-mark design. Shortly after the Bakelite Corporation was formed, in 1922, by the consolidation of the General Bakelite Company, the Redmanol Chemical Products Company, and the Condensite Company of America, it was deemed advisable to create a trade-mark symbol so that products made from "Bakelite" materials could be readily identified. The slogan, "The Material of a Thousand Uses," which had long been identified with the Redmanol products, was then being used in connection with the advertising of "Bakelite" materials. It was a matter of expressing this idea in a trade-mark design, and this immediately suggested the symbol for infinity which is defined as an infinite or very great quantity; boundless or immeasureable extension. Another element that was essential in the design was the letter "B" to designate "Bakelite" materials. Once the principal ingredients of the trade-mark had been decided upon, it was a matter of incorporating them in an appropriate design. The result is the Trefoil border in which is incorporated the capital "B" plus the sign for infinity.

Today the name "Bakelite" applies to the products manufactured and sold by the Bakelite Corporation, unit of Union Carbide and Carbon Corporation. Probably no material developed in this century has as many varied uses as "Bakelite."

FLIT SOLDIER

Reg. U. S. Pat. Off.
Reproduced Courtesy of Stanco Inc.

"FLIT" WAS first used as a trade-mark in 1923 by the Standard Oil Company (New Jersey). At that time liquid insecticides were just coming into general use. The demand for kerosene for lighting purposes had long been declining. This left a surplus of kerosene at the refineries. A liquid insecticide could be made by mixing kerosene and pyrethrum extract, thereby utilizing the surplus kerosene.

The Standard Oil Company (New Jersey), then a marketing organization, decided to put such a product on the market and sought a desirable brand for it. The late Mr. C. A. Straw, then patent attorney for the company, after a long search for a suitable trade-mark, suddenly suggested the word "Flit" as associated with flies, against which the insecticide was to be used and also indicating the quickness with which the product would kill the flies.

The "Flit Soldier" is an integral part of the "Flit"

business. Its origin dates back to the fall of 1924, when the Ketterlimus Lithographic Company of Philadelphia produced a soldier design in a window display. The design was at once recognized as a desirable advertising character. Soon miniature soldiers featured every advertisement and shortly thereafter the "Flit Soldier" became a part of the "Flit" label.

In 1927, Stanco Inc. was organized as a subsidiary of the Standard Oil Company (New Jersey) and the "Flit" trade-mark, business, and good will was assigned to it.

"Flit" is now a universal household word and the "Flit Soldier" is one of the well known trade-mark characters.

BROMO-SELTZER

IT WAS behind the prescription counter of a small drug store at Annapolis, Maryland, that Isaac E. Emerson first conceived the idea of preparing an inexpensive remedy for headaches, something which would quickly aid the throng of sufferers who came to his pharmacy seeking relief. Captain Emerson, a native of North Carolina, was interested in the study of chemistry from boyhood. He spent some time at the University of North Carolina as instructor in chemistry. Later he took up pharmacy as his life work, and the experience gained in the laboratory was of great benefit to him in the experimental work which led to the development of "Bromo-Seltzer."

In 1888, he went to Baltimore and began making and selling "Bromo-Seltzer." Three years later the Emerson Drug Company, of Baltimore City, was incorporated, and from then on the business grew rapidly, due to Captain Emerson's dynamic energy and his appreciation of the value of advertising. He was one of the first to use testimonials and cartoons with humorous verses, which are so popular today.

The name, "Bromo-Seltzer," was coined, but there is no authentic record as to its origin. Emerson and his three early associates have been dead for some time.

The Emerson Drug Company has carried on the advertising policy of the company's founder, and the product "Bromo-Seltzer" is universally known.

RED HEART

Reg. U. S. Pat. Off.
Reproduced Courtesy of John Morrell & Co.

DURING THE last decade the business of making and selling dog food in this country has grown by leaps and bounds. It is now one of the largest selling items in the food industry. An outstanding name is "Red Heart." This name and the red heart symbol have been connected with dog food since John Morrell & Co., pork and beef packers, of Ottumwa, Iowa, started manufacturing the product, in 1932.

Morrell's first use of a heart trade-mark dates to 1897, when a heart which was yellow in color appeared on their smoked meat labels. Three years later they began using red heart labels, and for more than forty years these labels have been associated with the house of Morrell.

The business which became John Morrell & Co., began in Bradford, England, in 1827, and spanned the Atlantic in 1865. For a time, packing plants were operated in Canada and later in Chicago. In 1877, the company opened a plant in Ottumwa, Iowa. It was the location of this plant in "the heart of Iowa's world-famed corn belt" which prompted the adoption of the heart trade-mark. For many years that phrase was used as an advertising slogan, but when the company began expanding with packing plants outside of Iowa, the slogan was dropped, although the red heart emblem continued to be featured.

Dog Biscuits and Kibbled Dog Food also carry the "Red Heart" trade-mark and are supplementary items in the Red Heart Dog Food line. It is estimated that "Red Heart" canned dog food is today the largest seller in the field.

SINGER

THE NAME, "Singer," in nearly every country in the world is synonymous with the sewing machine. It received its name from Isaac Merritt Singer, who, with his partner, Edward Clark, made and marketed the first practical sewing machine, in 1851. Mr. Singer was not the sole inventor of the sewing machine, but with his patents and those purchased and assembled by his firm, the sewing machine was made possible. The first few machines were produced in a small shop in Boston, Massachusetts, by the firm of I. M. Singer and Company.

The business began in a small way, the first year employing only twenty-five machinists and selling about three hundred machines. Expansion was rapid, and soon a factory and main office was established in New York. In 1863, the partnership was merged into a corporation, the Singer Manufacturing Company (of New York) which ten years later became a New Jersey corporation under the same name.

Within twenty-five years after the sewing machine was placed on the market, its yearly sales amounted to over half a million machines. The development of sewing machines for industrial purposes has added materially to its growth. The Singer Company in recent years has manufactured and sold other products, such as irons, vacuum cleaners, etc., under the name "Singer."

The Singer Company is now a world-wide organization, with factories and sales outlets in many different countries. It is said that the name, "Singer," is advertised in more foreign languages than any other trade name.

THE GREATEST NAME IN RUBBER
WINGFOOT——THE GOODYEAR SYMBOL

Reg. U. S. Pat. Off.
Courtesy of The Goodyear Tire & Rubber Company

PROBABLY THE first public announcement of the slogan, "The Greatest Name in Rubber," appeared in *The Saturday Evening Post* in December, 1927. The idea behind the slogan was to link Goodyear, the manufacturer, with Charles Goodyear, the inventor.

One hundred and one years ago Charles Goodyear invented the process of vulcanization and thus made rubber useful to mankind. The life of Mr. Goodyear was truly an amazing example of perseverance that neither disaster nor seeming disgrace could conquer. Calamities seemed to pursue him all through life—ill health, extreme poverty, and imprisonment for debts were a few of the blows that fate dealt him, but in spite of everything he persisted in his work and faith in his objective. As a youth, he began his experiments with rubber, which were to continue through many vicissitudes during most of his life. It took years of work before he finally discovered the process of heating for perfecting rubber, which he called "vulcanization," for Vulcan, mythological diety of fire. Goodyear's patent on this was issued to him in June, 1844. There followed six years of litigation which he finally won with the help of Daniel Webster. Unsuccessful in his attempt to get patent rights in England, Goodyear went on to France. There he was thrown in jail for debt and it was in a cold cell that his son finally found him to give him his freedom and the Cross of the Legion of Honor in recognition of his invention. He died in 1860 owing $200,000, but royalties from his invention erased the debt and a substantial sum was left to his family.

The Goodyear Tire & Rubber Company, Inc., was founded in August, 1898, and was named in honor of the inventor, Charles Goodyear. It is fitting that the inventor's name should be used by the largest rubber company in the world. Truly the name Goodyear is "The Greatest Name in Rubber."

Why does the "Wingfoot" emblem appear so frequently in the middle of the word Goodyear? And what is the origin of this famous symbol? The story dates back to the year 1900, when executives of the company were searching for a suitable trade-mark to distinguish the name Goodyear from Goodrich, since the names were so similar, and between Goodyear, the tire company, and other Goodyear concerns, which manufactured raincoats and other rubber products. Mr. F. A. Seiberling, then president of the Goodyear Company, had in his home in Akron, on a newel post of the stairway, a gilded statue, perched on tiptoe, of that famous god of mythology known to the ancient Greeks as Hermes and to the Romans as Mercury. Mr. Seiberling felt that the statue embodied many of the characteristics for which Goodyear products were known. A meeting of the Goodyear executives to discuss the idea of a trade-mark was held at the Seiberling home, and it was there decided to use the "Wingfoot"—the winged foot of Mercury —as the Goodyear trade-mark. Mercury is best known as the swift messenger of the gods of mythology, and the idea of speed had much to do with the selection of the symbol, but also it is as a herald of good tidings to tire users everywhere that the Goodyear "Wingfoot" now stands in the minds of the people of the world.

TRUTH IN ADVERTISING

IT IS impossible to say that on such a day in such a year "Truth in Advertising" was adopted by the advertising interests of the country as a slogan under which they were preparing to battle for higher standards of advertising. The truth movement, while not known as such in the early years, is, in fact, almost as old as organized advertising itself. As early as 1906, the leaders were discussing the problems of false advertising, and endeavoring to seek a solution for such practices. The sentiment was gradually crystallizing in 1910, when a federation of advertising associations held a national convention in Omaha, and adopted resolutions condemning misstatements and exaggerations, and especially criticizing publications which accepted misleading and obscene advertising. There was much discussion in that year and the next regarding "Honesty in Advertising," and that phrase, in fact, was the keynote of their 1911 convention.

Dallas, where the 1912 convention was held, claims credit for originating the actual slogan, "Truth in Advertising," and although there is nothing in the records to indicate a formal adoption of the slogan, the phrase began to appear frequently in the articles and records of the association's activities, following the convention. The Publicity Committee, feeling the need of a symbol for the movement, adopted, in January, 1913, what is now known as the "Truth" emblem—a circle with the name of the national organization lettered around the outer circumference, and within the inner circle the word "Truth" spread across a reproduction of the Western Hemisphere.

The "Truth" emblem, blazing forth from the largest electric sign ever erected in Baltimore up to that time, welcomed the advertisers at their convention in 1913, and it was at Baltimore that representatives from the advertising agencies, agricultural publications, directories, general advertisers, magazines, newspapers, outdoor advertising, printing and engraving, religious press, retail advertisers, technical publications, trade press, and special advertising, signed a pledge fostering truth in advertising, known as the "Baltimore Truth Declaration." Following the convention these various groups adopted individual Standards of Practice to enforce "Truth in Advertising" in their respective fields. Today the slogan is firmly entrenched in the activities and objectives of the Advertising Federation of America and its local affiliated Advertising Clubs.

Reg. U. S. Pat. Off.
Courtesy of Rock of Ages Corporation

THE TITLE of a famous hymn became a trade name. Prior to the use of the "Rock of Ages" name to memorials and memorial products, the granite produced by Boutwell, Milne & Varnum (predecessors of the Rock of Ages Corporation) at Barre, Vermont, was known as Dark Barre granite. Credit for supplying the appropriate name, "Rock of Ages," is given to Walter A. Myers.

Dark Barre granite was well accepted by the trade, but the producers were desirous of informing the ultimate buyers of memorials as to the merits of their product, and engaged Mr. Myers, an advertising man of Burlington, Vermont, to prepare a consumer-advertising booklet. While working on the assignment, the hymn, "Rock of Ages," caught his imagination as a possible name. At first the advertising agency was concerned as to how religious people might feel about the hymn being used for commercial purposes, but after due consideration, the agency recommended its adoption as a trade name. The company's acceptance was instant. It was registered as a trade-mark in 1914.

Rock of Ages Corporation is the largest memorial manufacturer in the world and its product is the oldest nationally advertised, and probably the best known, product of the Green Mountain State.

CANADA DRY

CLEOPATRA, BY dissolving a crushed pearl in wine causing it to sparkle and bubble, made the first carbonated type beverage. The first of the modern sparkling drinks was made by Thomas Speakman, a Philadelphia druggist, in the era following the American Revolution. By developing a crude but effective way of carbonating water, Speakman made a drink which gained wide popularity for its health properties. Later he added flavor to his sparkling water to improve the taste and thereby laid the foundation of the soft drink industry of today.

The original formula for ginger ale is credited to an Englishman, Nicholas Paul. The formula, however, for a dry ginger ale now known as "Canada Dry" was created by J. J. McLaughlin, a Canadian chemist. After sixteen years of experimenting in a small plant at Toronto he perfected his ginger ale in 1906. From the very beginning the product met an enthusiastic reception.

In 1914, J. J. McLaughlin, Ltd., was formed and the trade-mark, "Canada Dry," was officially adopted. The name was obviously chosen because the product was a dry ginger ale and made in Canada. Seven years later a selling agency was established in New York City and "Canada Dry" was introduced to the United States. The business expanded rapidly and, in 1932, Sparkling Water was added to the "Canada Dry" line.

It is estimated that Canada Dry Ginger Ale, Inc., is today the world's largest manufacturer of ginger ale.

CAMEL

Old Joe
*Reproduced Courtesy of R. J. Reynolds
Tobacco Company*

IF SPACE permitted, stories could be included on many famous trade-marks in the tobacco industry. A roll call of a few of the most prominent are: Camel, Fatima, Lucky Strike, Old Gold, Bull Durham, Chesterfield, Dukes Mixture, Prince Albert, Velvet, Horse Shoe, and Star. Some of these trade-marks originated many years ago.

This industry is perhaps more slogan-minded than any other. In fact, nearly every advertising campaign brings forth a new slogan. The best known include, "They satisfy," "I'd walk a mile for a Camel," "It's toasted."

"Camel" is one of the best known trade-marks, and here is the story of the original camel:

The trade-mark originated from Old Joe, the famous Barnum & Bailey Circus dromedary who was killed a few years ago in a railroad wreck at Bridgeport, Connecticut.

"Camel" cigarettes were first marketed in the fall of 1913. The blend had been decided upon and it had been agreed that the new cigarette should be called "Camel" and that the picture of a camel should adorn the package in which the new cigarettes were to be sold.

Right at this psychological time, the Barnum & Bailey Circus played in Winston-Salem, North Carolina, where "Camel" cigarettes are made. Circus day in the South is an event, and the employees of the R. J. Reynolds factories were released for the day so they could attend the circus.

An employee, now an important officer of the company, saw Old Joe and realized his picture would make an ideal trade-mark for the new "Camel" cigarette. Going to an official of the circus, he asked permission to photograph Old Joe. "We haven't got time for such foolishness," replied the circus man. But when the circus management was informed that R. J. Reynolds' factories had given all employees a holiday so they could see the circus, consent was given for the camel to be photographed. The resulting picture has been used ever since in connection with "Camel" cigarettes.

Old Joe, as a circus performer, was seen by thousands, and his picture, as a cigarette trade-mark, is familiar to millions.

DON'T WRITE—TELEGRAPH

NOT ALL famous slogans originate in the head office. Like Socrates, whose birthplace was claimed by many cities, the slogan, "Don't Write—Telegraph," has several claimants.

The slogan is said to have appeared for the first time on the windows of Western Union offices between 1917 and 1919, and is reported to have been used simultaneously at such widely separated places as Boston, Philadelphia, and Lewiston, Idaho.

The records of the Western Union Telegraph Company disclose that the company first began using the slogan as an advertising feature in February, 1920. About the same time it made its first appearance as a standard part of the company's window displays.

For two decades the simple effective phrase, "Don't Write—Telegraph," has been the outstanding communication slogan in this country.

PIGGLY WIGGLY

A YOUNG wholesale grocery salesman began to think about a more economical and time saving method of selling foodstuffs to the customer at retail. He saw dozens of impatient customers waiting their turn before a counter, many of them too timid to demand being waited on in their proper turn. He saw these same stores, on slack days, with idle clerks standing around waiting.

And then the idea was born. The idea of self-service—of permitting the customer to wait on herself—to choose what items she desired as quickly or as leisurely as she wished.

So, in September, 1916, the grocery salesman, Clarence Saunders, opened his first self-service store in Memphis, Tennessee. Its success was immediate, even spectacular. Within two months the crowds became so great that prospective customers were given admission cards on the street, and had to await their turn to get in to spend their money.

And then Saunders, with a stroke of genius, hit upon a name for his store that has rung down the corridors of grocery history for twenty-five years— the name, "Piggly Wiggly." It was taken from the way in which his mother told him as a child the nursery tale how a certain "piggly wiggly went to market."

The Piggly Wiggly Corporation was formed, and

by the end of the first year over fifty "Piggly Wiggly" stores were doing a land office business. By 1922, there were more than six hundred such stores coining money. Alas, too much money for the good of Saunders. This seemingly inexhaustible stream of shining, fresh money apparently made him forget the old adage about the shoemaker sticking to his last, and the groceryman to his onions. He became involved in Wall Street speculations, the result of which was that, in 1923, he lost control of the wonderful merchandising machine he had started. Saunders, however, had created something lasting—the self-service grocery store.

Under new management the growth of "Piggly Wiggly" stores continued. Today there are thousands of retail groceries operating under a franchise and the name of "Piggly Wiggly."

PARIS—NO METAL CAN TOUCH YOU

A. STEIN & COMPANY, manufacturers of a world famous line of garters, suspenders, and belts, was organized in 1887. These products are sold under the trade-mark, "Paris." The name, "Paris," was chosen because of its style connotation, and was registered as a trade-mark in 1909. Names which are geographic in character are very often difficult to sustain as trade-marks. The name "Paris," however, in this instance being used arbitrarily and not in its natural meaning, was held to be a valid trade-mark.

The well-known phrase, "No Metal Can Touch You," made its appearance a few years after the company adopted "Paris" as a trade-mark. They were the first to manufacture a type of garter in which none of the metal parts could touch the wearer. This comfort feature is a potent sales factor which the slogan reflects.

The company is a firm believer in slogans. For its free-swinging suspenders it uses, "Can't Skid off the Shoulders," and for its belts, "Tops for your Trousers."

From style and comfort standpoints, A. Stein & Company appear to have covered the ground by the adoption of the trade-mark, "Paris," and the slogan, "No Metal Can Touch You."

THE RED CROSS EMBLEM

THE ORIGIN of the use of the "Red Cross Emblem" by Johnson & Johnson, dates back before there was an humanitarian American Red Cross organization in this country. It has been continuously used by Johnson & Johnson and its predecessor founders (the Johnson brothers) since about 1874. The "Red Cross" trade-mark covers their entire line of surgical dressings and allied products. They also extensively use the name, "Red Cross."

The international Red Cross movement was started at Geneva in 1863 and a year later twenty-six countries met in Switzerland and adopted a white flag with a red cross as its emblem. In 1881, an American Red Cross organization was started in this country. The American organization was incorporated by an Act of Congress in 1905. The Act creating The American National Red Cross, expressly prohibited anyone from using the words, "Red Cross" or the "Red Cross Emblem" for the purpose of trade or as an advertisement to induce the sale of any article, or in connection with any business, except those that had used the words, "Red Cross," and the emblem prior to January 5, 1905.

Johnson & Johnson, having used the emblem and the words, "Red Cross," many years before the passage of the Act, was not affected by the legislation. There were other companies that had used "Red Cross" and the emblem in other lines of business which were also not affected by the Act of 1905, but none were outstanding in their particular field as were Johnson & Johnson.

The "Red Cross Emblem" of Johnson & Johnson products for many years has stood for the world's largest manufacturers of surgical dressings.

THE  MONOGRAM

GE, GM, AT&T, RCA, MGM, NBC, JM, TWA, NCR, and P&G are some of the familiar initials of great national organizations. In many instances, initials are registered trade-marks. Perhaps the best known is the "G. E." Monogram. It has been the emblem of General Electric products since the beginning of this century and has appeared in connection with more different kinds of products than any other emblem in the world. It may be seen on the massive electric equipment at Boulder Dam; on the modern stream-lined engines streaking across the country; on power plants; on radio transmitters; on oil burners, refrigerators, radios, Mazda lamps, fans, clocks, etc.

From time to time the "G. E." Monogram has been accompanied with effective slogans and phrases, such as, "The Initials of a Friend" and "The House of Magic."

Thomas A. Edison, the inventor, was one of the founders of a company in 1878 which later merged with other companies to form the General Electric Company.

ARM & HAMMER

A BARED ARM with hand grasping the handle of a hammer in a striking position is one of America's most familiar trade-marks. There is very little information available as to the origin of the famous "Arm & Hammer" symbol. Several of the present executives of Church & Dwight Co., Inc., the present owners of the trade-mark, are of the third generation of the founders.

In 1846, Dr. Austin Church and his brother-in-law, Mr. John Dwight, started making and selling baking soda (bicarbonate of soda) in New York City. They went along together for about fifteen years when it was agreed they would separate and two firms were formed, John Dwight & Co., and Church & Co. The "Arm & Hammer" brand was first packed by the latter company in a small plant in Brooklyn. The company had many labels, but the "Arm & Hammer" became so popular that all the rest were discarded. It has been continuously used as a trade-mark for nearly seventy years, although it was not registered until 1897.

In 1896, Church & Dwight Co. succeeded to the business of Church & Co. The symbol is now only used on two of the company's products, baking soda, or bicarbonate of soda, and washing soda, commonly called sal soda.

"Arm & Hammer" is universally known as the trade-mark for products used daily in millions of homes.

KEEP THAT SCHOOLGIRL COMPLEXION

PERHAPS NO poster advertising ever received more favorable comment than Clarence Underwood's paintings of beautiful young girls, accompanied by the phrase, "Keep That Schoolgirl Complexion." While this phrase had been used earlier with other posters, it was the Underwood series of paintings that made the slogan famous.

An executive of The Palmolive Company, Mr. Charles S. Pearce, was inspired by a picture of a beautiful young girl which was to be used in an advertisement of Palmolive Cold Cream. The portrayal of a lovely complexion in the picture suggested to him the headline, "Keep That Schoolgirl Complexion." The records of the present owners, Colgate-Palmolive-Peet Company, disclose that the slogan first made its appearance in magazine copy in 1917, a few years after the phrase was coined by Mr. Pearce. It caught the public fancy almost immediately and has been in use ever since.

Although this slogan has been before the public only about two decades, the origin of the various companies which make up the present company date far into the past. The Colgate Company started in 1806; in 1864, Burdette J. Johnson set up a small soap and candle business which later became The Palmolive Company in 1916; The Peet Brothers Company was organized in 1872; Palmolive Company and Peet Brothers merged to become The Palmolive-Peet Company; the Colgate Company and The Palmolive-Peet Company became merged in 1928 and became the present Colgate-Palmolive-Peet Company.

BULL DURHAM

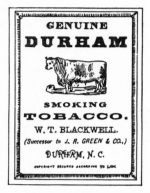

Copy of original trade-mark registration

THE PICTURE of a Durham bull helped build a city and contributed to the growth of the tobacco industry in this country.

Sometime in the late fifties the North Carolina Railroad was laid across the farm of Dr. Bartlett Durham, in Orange County, North Carolina. A station was established there, and called Durham Station. This spot shortly became the seat of a small tobacco factory, a blacksmith shop, a tavern, and the residence of two or three families. It remained an insignificant place until after the Civil War. It then grew steadily under the effects of a very prosperous tobacco business which had risen there. Durham is now a thriving city of over fifty thousand inhabitants, and is known as the "Tobacco City."

A tobacco factory was established at Durham Station in 1860 by the firm of Morris & Wright. They principally manufactured plug tobacco, but utilized the clippings and waste tobacco by putting them in little bags and disposing of it as smoking tobacco. Wright sold his interest to his partner, and joined the Confederate Army. Shortly thereafter, J. R. Green became the successor to the business of Morris & Wright. The preying of the armies of Sherman and Johnston on Green's tobacco toward the close of the Civil War helped Green's business materially, for after the armies disbanded orders came from all parts of the Union for "smoking tobacco in the small bags." His business grew rapidly. He adopted as his brand the words "Durham Smoking Tobacco," and used the figure of a shorthorn Durham bull as a symbol of the word "Durham." A full-sized painting of such a bull was placed broad-side upon the factory, in conspicuous view of the railroad, as an advertisement of his business to all travelers. The town of Durham gradually came to be associated with the picture as the "Home of the Bull."

The "Durham Bull," now universally known, is one of the earliest registered trade-marks, No. 122 (1870).

The "Bull Durham" tobacco business has changed ownership many times. Today it is owned by the American Tobacco Company. It is now, and has been since the Civil War, one of the leading brands of smoking tobacco in the world. Recently, Mrs. Doris Duke Cromwell, heiress of the Duke tobacco fortune, for sentimental purposes, resurrected from a barn the original bronze bull which was the model for the old "Bull Durham" label, and placed it on the beautiful grounds at her home in Somerville, New Jersey.

TOASTMASTER

The original "pop-up" type of automatic electric toaster was invented by Charles Strite. In 1920, the Waters-Genter Company, of Minneapolis, began marketing the toaster as the "Strite Automatic Toaster." About four years later, the company's advertising agent, the Mitchell Advertising Agency, Inc., coined the name "Toastmaster" as the trademark and trade name for the toaster. It was registered in 1925.

The name, "Toastmaster," is doubly effective—it is not only apropos for a toasting device, but signifies leadership, the presider at a banquet.

Max McGraw, in 1925, purchased the capital stock of the Waters-Genter Company, and four years later the business and the famous trade-mark, "Toastmaster," were acquired by the present owner, the McGraw Electric Company.

The trade-mark has been extended to other electrical appliances, such as waffle irons, flat irons, coffeemakers, grills, dishes, electric water heaters, etc. The company's products have maintained the leadership set by "Toastmaster."

SCRIPPS-HOWARD LIGHTHOUSE

*"Give Light and the People Will Find
Their Own Way"*

ALBUQUERQUE, NEW MEXICO, is about as far away
from a lighthouse as any city in this country, yet
the well-known Scripps-Howard Lighthouse trade-
mark and the slogan, "Give Light and the People
Will Find Their Own Way," had its origin in that
Southwest inland city.

In April, 1922, Carl C. Magee began publishing,
in Albuquerque, *The New Mexico State Tribune*
(now *The Albuquerque Tribune*). A few years later,
Mr. Magee began heading his editorial column with
the phrase, "Turning on the Light," and in smaller
type beneath, "Give Light and the People Will Find
Their Own Way." The records are not clear as to
whether Magee, or an employee of the Scripps-

Howard newspapers, originated the Lighthouse trade-mark, but there is no doubt that Mr. Magee's slogan was the inspiration for the lighthouse. It made its first appearance in *The New Mexico State Tribune* on April 25, 1927.

At the suggestion of Robert P. Scripps, the Lighthouse design was registered as a trade-mark for the New York Telegram Corporation on November 1, 1927, and its use later was extended to all Scripps-Howard newspapers.

Today the famous Lighthouse trade-mark and the slogan, "Give Light and the People Will Find Their Own Way," is the emblem and motto for the Scripps-Howard chain of newspapers, extending from coast to coast, with a total circulation of approximately two million.

B. V. D.

THE TRADE-MARK, "B. V. D.," is familiar to the natives along the gold coast of Africa, who speak no English and still use primitive washing methods such as beating clothes against rock at the sea. It is known to the "Wild man from Borneo," and to the "Bulls" and "Bears" of Wall Street. In fact, it is perhaps the best known initial trade-mark in the world.

The letters, "B.V.D.," represent the initials of the last names of three men, *B*radley, *V*oorhies and *D*ay, associated with the business in 1876.

The trade-mark first became famous in connection with men's underwear. It is now associated with other garments such as shirts, pajamas, robes, sport-wear, etc. The B. V. D. Corporation, with main offices in New York City, is at the present time the proud owner of this universally known trade-mark.

Before "B. V. D." athletic underwear was introduced, getting into the old type of undergarments was an acrobatic feat. With the introduction of the new, comfortable, loose-fitting underwear came a very catchy, expressive slogan, "Next to myself, I like B. V. D. best." This phrase, for more than two decades, has been constantly and extensively used in connection with the advertising and sale of "B. V. D." products.

ASCAP
"Justice for Genius"

"ASCAP" IS THE alphabetical designation by which the American Society of Composers, Authors, and Publishers is known in the musical profession and industry. It is a voluntary non-profit association of composers, authors, and publishers of musical works. The society was organized in 1914 by the late Victor Herbert and a few of his contemporaries. Unable as individuals to protect their copyrighted compositions against infringement by illegal public performance for profit, they recognized the necessity for an organization which could act for them collectively, as the only means of acquiring protection.

The revenue which "ASCAP" collects for licenses issued to commercial users of music for public performances, after the expenses of operation have been deducted, is divided amongst the members of the society and of the foreign societies with which "ASCAP" is affiliated. The membership of the entire group exceeds forty-five thousand of the men and women who write most of the music which the world enjoys. The organization is actively engaged in various kinds of charities for its members.

In recent years, the American Society of Composers, Authors, and Publishers has extensively and consistently used the slogan, "Justice for Genius." The phrase originated from an editorial under that caption by Dr. James Francis Cooke, editor of *The Etude,* appearing in November, 1937, in that widely circulated musical magazine. In Dr. Cooke's editorial he gave, as an illustration, the tragic financial condition of Franz Schubert, who, upon his death in 1928, left an estate of not more than ten or fifteen dollars, notwithstanding the fact that the aggregate revenue of Schubert's music should have made him one of the weathiest men of his time. Dr. Cooke suggested something more substantial than a few plaudits for the music of a Schubert, a Mozart, or a Stephen Foster; in other words—"Justice for Genius."

GIVE WHITMAN'S CHOCOLATES
IT'S THE THOUGHTFUL THING TO DO

THE WORLD-FAMOUS confectionery business of Whitman's began in 1842, when Stephen Whitman opened a modest little confectionery shop in Philadelphia. Most fine candies at that time were imported from Europe, but Whitman believed that candy, good as any that ever crossed the Atlantic, could be made right here in the United States.

Stephen Whitman made his own candies, waited on customers himself. And his fame soon spread afar. Those were the days when stage-coaches rolled the highway between New York, Philadelphia, Baltimore, and Washington. Happy indeed was the traveller who was able to bring back from Philadelphia a box of "those new Whitman's candies" as a souvenir of his stay in William Penn's town.

From the first, the makers of Whitman's Chocolates have been strong believers in the power of advertising. Newspapers, magazines, and other media have been used to make the name and quality of Whitman's known to the far corners of the earth. The cross-stitch Sampler package, which Whitman's introduced to the public in 1912, is believed to be the only box of candy universally known, and asked for by its own name.

The sales slogan, "Give Whitman's Chocolates— it's the thoughtful thing to do," had its inception in

1933. In these depression years, Whitman's wanted to drive home the fact that hospitality, thoughtfulness, and the graceful art of keeping the social fences in good repair had not been lost with the stock market slump.

GREYHOUND

A CASUAL remark by a Wisconsin innkeeper suggested the name "Greyhound" for the world's largest motor coach company.

At the head of The Greyhound Corporation in Chicago, is Mr. C. E. Wickman, president of the corporation and founder of the Greyhound lines. The rise of Mr. Wickman and Greyhound lines is synonymous. The origin of the organization goes back to 1914, when Mr. Wickman, then employed as a diamond drill operator on the Mesaba iron range at Hibbing, Minnesota, utilizing a seven-passenger Hupmobile, converted the car into a bus capable of seating ten passengers and started carrying the iron miners from Hibbing to the iron pits, which was a distance of six miles. The fare charged was fifteen cents one way and twenty-five cents for a round trip. The first day's receipts netted the sum of $2.25. A few weeks later, Mr. Wickman was unable to care for the business coming his way so he took on a partner, purchased another car, converted it into a bus, added more routes and expanded rapidly. The phenomenal growth of the Greyhound lines in the past two decades is common knowledge to all.

Here is the story of the origin of the name "Greyhound," in the words of Mr. Wickman the founder:

"In the early days when we first started operating a bus line, there were no commercially made buses, and we lengthened out seven-passenger Packard and White touring cars, adding two extra seats in the middle, making room for ten passengers in addition to the driver. On account of the dusty road conditions in that part of the country (northern Minnesota) in those days, we painted these vehicles battleship grey. In the early 1920's, our line was extended down through Wisconsin, and in the town of Fond du Lac, which was a centrally located point, the buses made a stop at the local hotel. There were two buses used on this run, both of them lengthened out touring cars and painted battleship grey. On seeing these buses one day, the hotel keeper, whose name has since escaped me, made a chance remark that these buses looked just like 'Greyhounds.' The name stuck. At first it was attached only to these two particular buses, but later on became adopted as the operating name, or trade name, of the fleet, and subsequently as the name of the corporation."

THE WATCH OF RAILROAD ACCURACY

THE HAMILTON Watch Company chose its famous slogan, "The Watch of Railroad Accuracy," from a phrase used by a railroad man in a letter to the company testifying as to the uncanny time his watch kept.

In 1892, the company began operations in Lancaster, Pennsylvania. Its sole product was railroad watches, built to meet a growing demand for accurate timepieces for railroaders. In those days, safety devices were crude; automatic appliances, such as we have today, were unknown; railroad accidents were frequent, particularly where tracks crossed. Attention was centered on watches, because in several investigations of wrecks, blame was placed on faulty timepieces in the engineers' pockets. Railroads began to establish official railroad watches and time inspection services. Very rigid specifications were written for watches to comply with the official service. The Hamilton watch was built according to these specifications. All through the 1890's the company advertised extensively to railroad men through their employee and brotherhood publications.

The watch clicked with the railroaders and a phrase used by a railroad man clicked with the Hamilton Watch Company—"The Watch of Railroad Accuracy." In 1908, when the company began advertising a general line of watches, the phrase, which had become a slogan in their railroad advertising, was used in advertising nationally all their watches.

At the present time, after more than forty years' tested service, the Hamilton Watch Company consistently uses the slogan which meant so much during the country's railroad expansion era.

SAY IT WITH FLOWERS

For NEARLY two decades "Say It With Flowers" has been an effective slogan of the florists in this country. No industry has a phrase so universally used by its members. It appears in nearly all of their advertising—on florists' windows, on signs, stationery, flower boxes, etc. In fact, the phrase has become synonymous with the floral shop.

Henry Penn, a florist of Boston, Massachusetts, was not only the first to use the slogan in his business, but he had perhaps more to do with originating it than anyone else. In the early 1920's, when Mr. Penn was chairman of the National Publicity Committee of the Society of American Florists, he was discussing one day possibilities of a slogan for the industry with the late Major P. K. O'Keefe, head of an advertising agency. The Major suggested "Flowers are words that even a babe can understand," which he got from a book of poems. Mr. Penn thought it was too long, and as it was considered, along with other phrases, the Major said, "Why, you can say it with flowers in so many"—bang! went Mr. Penn's hand on the table, for his ears had caught the words "Say it with flowers," and he instantly decided there was the slogan.

The reason for the popularity of the phrase is that almost any emotion can be expressed in the language of flowers; love, sympathy, felicitations, gratitude, congratulations, romance, and memory. No matter what the intended message is, flowers will express it perfectly, and more and more people have come to realize this through the continued advertising of the slogan, "Say It With Flowers."

SMITH BROTHERS

Reg. U. S. Pat. Off.
Reproduced Courtesy of Smith Brothers, Inc.

NOW, LAST but not least, we come to the noted Smith Brothers. The list would not be complete without "Trade" and "Mark" flourishing their luxuriant beards. You may have heard them on the air, seen them in vaudeville, and recognized them in cartoons. They seem a little like Santa Claus—widely impersonated but not real human beings. However, the Smith Brothers actually lived, and here is their story:

James Smith moved his family from Canada to Poughkeepsie, New York, in 1847. He had three sons, James, William, and Andrew. William and Andrew are the ones known today as "Trade" and "Mark," respectively. In 1847, they were mere boys; they hadn't yet acquired the whiskers.

James Smith and Sons first ran a small restaurant, which grew nicely. The New York Central Railroad was being built, and there were plenty of people to feed. Old Commodore Vanderbilt himself occasionally dropped in at the Smith Restaurant. (This same restaurant, much enlarged, is still in operation in Poughkeepsie.)

Later, a modest confectionery line was added, and the cough drops appeared. Father James started producing them in a small way in the kitchen of his restaurant and they were sold on the streets of Poughkeepsie by his sons, William and Andrew.

The business grew, as the fame of the drops spread up and down the Hudson Valley. James Smith died and William (Trade) and Andrew (Mark) inherited the business. Under their guidance, the drops were placed on sale throughout the surrounding country. And then competition reared its head. In order to identify their own product, the Brothers Smith, by this time in possession of their flowing beards, realized that a distinctive trade-mark was needed.

They decided to place their own pictures on the glass bowls they had given their dealers for displaying the cough drops on store counters. They also printed their pictures on the small envelopes which they furnished dealers for convenience in handling sales. This method still being unsatisfactory, the present pocket package, also carrying the picture of the Smith Brothers was developed. This package was one of the first instances of uniform packaging for a popular priced product.

With the new cartons, Smith Brothers Cough Drops were sold more widely. The faces of "Trade" and "Mark" were among the best known countenances of their time. William resembled General Grant and Andrew wore the same free-flowing style of beard as Edwin M. Stanton, Secretary of War in Lincoln's Cabinet.

The business is still run by William's descendants; his two grandsons, William and Robert, head "Smith Brothers, Inc."

GETTING AND SPENDING:
The Consumer's Dilemma
An Arno Press Collection

Babson, Roger W[ard]. **The Folly of Instalment Buying.** 1938

Bauer, John. **Effective Regulation of Public Utilities.** 1925

Beckman, Theodore N. and Herman C. Nolen. **The Chain Store Problem.** 1938

Berridge, William A., Emma A. Winslow and Richard A. Flinn. **Purchasing Power of the Consumer.** 1925

Borden, Neil H. **The Economic Effects of Advertising.** 1942

Borsodi, Ralph. **The Distribution Age.** 1927

Brainerd, J. G[rist], editor. **The Ultimate Consumer.** 1934

Carson, Gerald. **Cornflake Crusade.** [1957]

Cassels, John M[acIntyre]. **A Study of Fluid Milk Prices.** 1937

Caveat Emptor. 1976

Cherington, Paul Terry. **Advertising as a Business Force.** 1913

Clark, Evans. **Financing the Consumer.** 1933

Cook, James. **Remedies and Rackets:** The Truth About Patent Medicines Today. [1958]

Cover, John H[igson]. **Neighborhood Distribution and Consumption of Meat in Pittsburgh.** [1932]

Federal Trade Commission. **Chain Stores.** 1933

Ferber, Robert and Hugh G. Wales, editors. **Motivation and Market Behavior.** 1958

For Richer or Poorer. 1976

Grether, Ewald T. **Price Control Under Fair Trade Legislation.** 1939

Harding, T. Swann. **The Popular Practice of Fraud.** 1935

Haring, Albert. **Retail Price Cutting and Its Control by Manufacturers.** [1935]

Harris, Emerson P[itt]. **Co-operation:** The Hope of the Consumer. 1918

Hoyt, Elizabeth Ellis. **The Consumption of Wealth.** 1928

Kallen, Horace M[eyer]. **The Decline and Rise of the Consumer.** 1936

Kallet, Arthur and F. J. Schlink. **100,000,000 Guinea Pigs:** Dangers in Everyday Foods, Drugs, and Cosmetics. 1933

Kyrk, Hazel. **A Theory of Consumption.** [1923]

Laird, Donald A[nderson]. **What Makes People Buy.** 1935

Lamb, Ruth deForest. **American Chamber of Horrors:** The Truth About Food and Drugs. [1936]

Lambert, I[saac] E. **The Public Accepts:** Stories Behind Famous Trade-Marks, Names, and Slogans. [1941]

Larrabee, Carroll B. **How to Package for Profit.** 1935

Lough, William H. **High-Level Consumption.** 1935

Lyon, Leverett S[amuel]. **Hand-to-Mouth Buying.** 1929

Means, Gardiner C. **Pricing Power and the Public Interest.** [1962]

Norris, Ruby Turner. **The Theory of Consumer's Demand.** 1952

Nourse, Edwin G. **Price Making in a Democracy.** 1944

Nystrom, Paul H[enry]. **Economic Principles of Consumption.** [1929]

Pancoast, Chalmers Lowell. **Trail Blazers of Advertising.** 1926

Pasdermadjian, H[rant]. **The Department Store.** 1954

Pease, Otis. **The Responsibilities of American Advertising.** 1958

Peixotto, Jessica B[lanche]. **Getting and Spending at the Professional Standard of Living.** 1927

Radin, Max. **The Lawful Pursuit of Gain.** 1931

Reid, Margaret G. **Consumers and the Market.** 1947

Rheinstrom, Carroll. **Psyching the Ads.** [1929]

Rorty, James. **Our Master's Voice:** Advertising. [1934]

Schlink, F. J. **Eat, Drink and Be Wary.** [1935]

Seldin, Joseph J. **The Golden Fleece:** Selling the Good Life to Americans. [1963]

Sheldon, Roy and Egmont Arens. **Consumer Engineering.** 1932

Stewart, Paul W. and J. Frederic Dewhurst. **Does Distribution Cost Too Much?** 1939

Thompson, Carl D. **Confessions of the Power Trust.** 1932

U. S. National Commission on Food Marketing. **Food From Farmer to Consumer.** 1966

U. S. Senate Subcommittee on Anti-Trust and Monopoly of the Committee on the Judiciary. **Administered Prices.** 1963

Waite, Warren C[leland] and Ralph Cassady, Jr. **The Consumer and the Economic Order.** 1939

Washburn, Robert Collyer. **The Life and Times of Lydia E. Pinkham.** 1931

Wiley, Harvey W[ashington]. **The History of a Crime Against the Food Law.** [1929]

Wright, Richardson [Little]. **Hawkers and Walkers in Early America.** 1927

Zimmerman, Carle C[lark]. **Consumption and Standards of Living.** 1936